Essential New Zealand POEMS

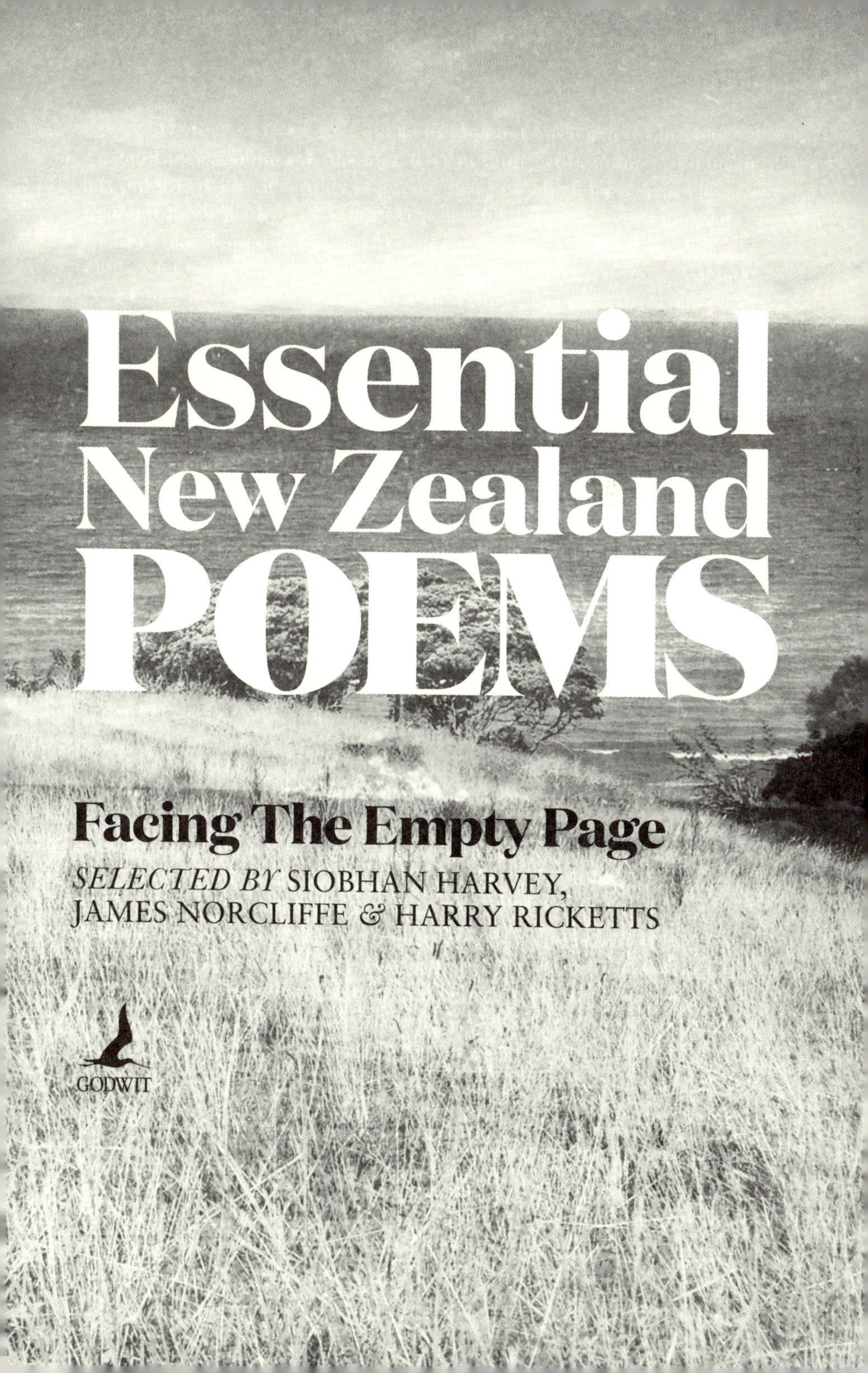

Essential New Zealand POEMS

Facing The Empty Page

SELECTED BY SIOBHAN HARVEY,
JAMES NORCLIFFE & HARRY RICKETTS

GODWIT

To New Zealand poets
past, present, and to come

Contents

Introduction 10

Fleur Adcock — Having Sex with the Dead 21
Johanna Aitchison — Letters from Japanese Kids 22
Raewyn Alexander — Old News Curling in the Sun 23
John Allison — Near Death Experience 24
Nick Ascroft — The Status of the Night 25
Tusiata Avia — Wild Dogs Under My Skirt 26
Stu Bagby — First Dance 28
Hinemoana Baker — As a Child 30
Serie Barford — Mongolian Spots 31
Sarah Jane Barnett — When the Sister Walks 32
James K. Baxter—Ode to Auckland 33
David Beach — Abandoned Novel 37
Tony Beyer — Cut Lilac 38
Peter Bland — Sorry, I'm a stranger here myself . . . 39
Jenny Bornholdt — Villanelle 42
Charles Brasch — World Without End 43
Diana Bridge — Jars, Bubble Bowls and Bottle Vases 44
Bub Bridger — A Christmas Wish 46
Sarah Broom — defrost the dog 48
Amy Brown — Baba Yaga 49
Diane Brown — Follow Me If You Will 50
James Brown — Needs Work 51
Owen Bullock — abstractions 54
Rachel Bush — She Is Lost 55
Kate Camp — Personal Effects 56
Alistair Te Ariki Campbell — Te Rauparaha in Old Age 57
Meg Campbell — My Countrywoman 59
Gordon Challis — Poem for Magda 60
Janet Charman — invigilator 61

Geoff Cochrane — The Last of Bashō 64
Glenn Colquhoun — To the girl who stood beside me at the checkout counter of Whitcoulls bookstore in Hamilton on Tuesday 65
Kay McKenzie Cooke — Feeding the Dogs 67
Allen Curnow — You Will Know When You Get There 68
Ruth Dallas — Photographs of Pioneer Women 70
Lynn Davidson — Cape Gooseberries 71
Stephanie de Montalk — Concrete 72
John Dickson — sleeper 78
Emily Dobson — *from* A Box of Bees 80
Lauris Edmond — Late Song 81
Murray Edmond — The Cold War 82
David Eggleton — Titirangi Considered as Wearable Art 83
Riemke Ensing — Hokianga Love Song 85
Rangi Faith — Advice to a Colonial Artist 88
Fiona Farrell — Fairytale 89
Cliff Fell — Alive 90
Jan FitzGerald — Cows Crossing 91
Joan Fleming — Armchair Talking to the Window 92
Janet Frame — The Place 93
Janis Freegard — Sapphire 94
Anne French — The Lady Fishermen 95
Rhian Gallagher — Salt Water Creek 96
Denis Glover — Towards Banks Peninsula 98
Paula Green — Two Minutes Westward 99
David Gregory — The Cruise 101
Bernadette Hall — The Lay Sister 102
Michael Harlow — And, Yes 104
Siobhan Harvey — Tooth 105
Dinah Hawken — The Tug of War 107
Helen Heath — Ripple 110
Jeffrey Paparoa Holman — *from* The Late Great Blackball Bridge Sonnets 111
Ingrid Horrocks — Light Between Houses 112

John Horrocks — WEATHER REPORT — FINE 113
David Howard — A SIMPLE CHRONOLOGY 114
Keri Hulme — WAITING ON THE LAUGHING OWL 117
Sam Hunt — MY FATHER TODAY 118
Jan Hutchison — UNWINDING MATARIKI'S HAIR 120
Kevin Ireland — PAINTING IN THE MANIOTOTO 122
Rob Jackaman — LEMONS (OFF SEASON) 123
Anna Jackson — BADMINTON 125
Michael Jackson — THE MOTHS 127
Helen Jacobs — VESSEL CONTAINING 128
Adrienne Jansen — DUNEDIN: PLAYING SCRABBLE WITH MY AUNT 129
Louis Johnson — THE LAST CANNIBAL 131
Mike Johnson — UP ON HIGH 134
Andrew Johnston — THE SUNFLOWER 135
Jan Kemp — SWIMMING 140
Anne Kennedy — I WAS A FEMINIST IN THE EIGHTIES 141
Fiona Kidman — MAKARA BEACH, SPRING 143
Koenraad Kuiper — *from* TALES 144
Leonard Lambert — A MORNING WALK IN THE LATER DAYS 146
Aleksandra Lane — SOLD OUT 147
Jessica Le Bas — TWO ANGELS 148
Michele Leggott — SLOW READER 149
Graham Lindsay — RIVER OF LOVE 151
Anna Livesey — AUTUMN DAY 153
Iain Lonie — PROPOSAL AT ALLANS BEACH 156
Rachel McAlpine — BEFORE THE FALL 158
Robert McLean — SPRINGTIME IN AMERICA 159
Frankie McMillan — DEVELOPING MY FATHER 160
Cilla McQueen — LIVING HERE 161
Margaret Mahy — BUBBLE TROUBLE 163
Vana Manasiadis — HECTIC HECTOR 166
Bill Manhire — KEVIN 169
Selina Tusitala Marsh — TWO NUDES ON A TAHITIAN BEACH, *1894* 170
Courtney Sina Meredith — HOMELAND 172

Karlo Mila — Eating Dark Chocolate and Watching Paul Holmes' Apology 173
David Mitchell — A Letter 178
Harvey Molloy — Battle of San Romano 179
Elizabeth Nannestad — Facing the Empty Page 181
Emma Neale — Well 184
John Newton — Opening the book 185
James Norcliffe — The Gentle Art of Manipulation 187
Gregory O'Brien — House and Children 188
John O'Connor — A Left Hook 190
Maris O'Rourke — On Being Told I'm To Be a Grandmother: a Villanelle 192
Peter Olds — Under the Dundas Street Bridge 193
Bob Orr — Calypso 195
Chris Orsman — A Colonial Farewell 196
Vincent O'Sullivan — Seeing You Asked 200
Alistair Paterson — Laying Your Ghost 202
Kiri Piahana-Wong — This is it 204
Sugu Pillay — St Heliers 206
Mark Pirie — Three Short Films (with '*Landscape*' included) 208
Vivienne Plumb — Vic's Dick 211
Lindsay Pope — Outpost 213
Jenny Powell — Love in the Early Winter 215
Joanna Preston — Parable of the Drought 216
Chris Price — Keeping Ravens 218
John Pule — *from* The Hurricane Love Songs 222
Sarah Quigley — To Waitemata Harbour 223
Maggie Rainey-Smith — At Katherine's Bay 224
Richard Reeve — Summer Wedding 226
Nicholas Reid — Bluff Seas 228
Helen Rickerby — *from* Abstract Internal Furniture 229
Harry Ricketts — The Necessity of Failure 230
Jack Ross — Trying to Write 232
Bill Sewell — By Ships We Live 233

Iain Sharp — The Ponsonby Strut 235
Kerrin P. Sharpe — Mining the Heart 237
Elizabeth Smither — Leaf Flurry Tram 238
C. K. Stead — Deconstructing the Rainbow Warrior 239
J. C. Sturm — Honestly 241
Robert Sullivan — Listen to the Rhythm of the Falling Rain 243
Apirana Taylor — Sad Joke on a Marae 246
Charlotte Trevella — The Red Dress 247
Chris Tse — In Which the Author Interviews a Dead Man 249
Brian Turner — Just This 251
Hone Tuwhare — Deep River Talk 252
Tim Upperton — Kindness 254
Rae Varcoe — My Hairdresser 255
Louise Wallace — I feel like I am having the world's heaviest baby 256
Ian Wedde — To Art and Praxis 257
Albert Wendt — Last Night 258
Tom Weston — The Sadness of Gifts 259
Pat White — Learning to Live Outdoors 260
Alison Wong — there's always things to come back to the kitchen for 261
Sue Wootton — Alpine 262
Sonja Yelich — wires 263
Ashleigh Young — Doors 264
Karen Zelas — Small Islands of Difference 266

Poet Biographies 270
Acknowledgements 307
About the Editors 314
Index of Titles 316

INTRODUCTION

It has been a heady time to be a poet in New Zealand over the last decade or two. The battles, the finger-wagging, the manifestos of the 1950s, 1960s and 1970s now seem as quaint and dated as paisley and flares. If fewer books and journals of poetry are being published than back then, electronic media, new technology and slams have tapped into new outlets and new audiences. Eclecticism rules.

Contemporary poetry can be personal and public, passionate and disengaged, complex and simple, formal and informal. It can be condensed or distilled, rambling or bardic. It can be serious and comic, sometimes in the same poem. It can be for the page, the stage, the blog, the chat-room, the CD, the DVD, the iPod, the mobile, the Kindle and the Kobo. Wherever and however it is accessed, New Zealand poetry takes its influences from the present, the past, from Asia and the Pacific, from Europe, from America . . . In short, with a magpie-like enthusiasm, it takes its influences from anywhere and everywhere.

This selection of 150 poems by 150 New Zealand poets is published to succeed the 2001 Godwit anthology *Essential New Zealand Poems*, edited by the late Lauris Edmond and Bill Sewell and now out of print. We decided to restrict each poet to a single poem, opening the way to voices not represented in Edmond's and Sewell's original selection (Glenn Colquhoun, Paula Green, Pat White, Kerrin P. Sharpe, Karlo Mila . . .) and to a range of even newer poets who have recently achieved or will soon achieve the milestone of their first collection: Helen Heath, Courtney Sina Meredith, Kiri Piahana-Wong, Chris Tse and Ashleigh Young. It is the editors' hope that this anthology as a whole will reflect 'headiness' — the variety, the sheer diversity of contemporary New Zealand poetry and the idiosyncratic flair of its practitioners. This is also the yardstick, we believe, by which these poems can be described as 'essential'.

Cumulatively, what is distilled by these 150 New Zealand poets and their New Zealand poems? What commonality exists in this anthology which might, for the reader, summon up an essence of what New Zealand poetry is? For a start, running through many of these poems is a powerful sense of place, of a distinctive New Zealand geography; and also, an acknowledgement of how our poets have engaged and continue to engage with the land: Allen Curnow in 'You Will Know When You Get There'; Fiona Kidman in 'Makara Beach, Spring'; Iain Lonie in 'Proposal at Allans Beach'; Keri Hulme in 'Waiting on the Laughing Owl'; John Newton in 'Opening the book'; John Horrocks in 'Weather Report'.

At the same time, Fleur Adcock's 'Having Sex with the Dead', James Brown's 'Needs Work', Kate Camp's 'Personal Effects', Jenny Bornholdt's 'Villanelle' and Alison Wong's 'there's always things to come back to the kitchen for', like many of the poems we have included, could have been written anywhere. But here too there is, in our view, an engagement with and a finger on the pulse of New Zealand, on its society, its culture and its mores — both as they are present and as they are evolving.

Even so, establishing 'essentialness' was problematic. 'Immediate impact' guided Lauris Edmond's and Bill Sewell's selection material, Sewell defining it thus: 'a poem had to present at least some aspect that made it instantly appealing to the heart and ear — to be memorable, or have a quality that would make the reader want to go back to it, preferably many times.'

The first *Essential New Zealand Poems* made no mention of the word 'essential' except in its title, and, wisely perhaps, made no attempt to tease out what might or might not be labelled an 'essential New Zealand poem'. In revisiting Edmond's and Sewell's collection, we too found that the word 'essential' posed problems — semantic, philosophical and practical. The most obvious of these is one of definition. The simplest definition of 'essential' is 'absolutely necessary; indispensable'. But by that reckoning no poems, not even Shakespeare's or Homer's, can be thought 'essential' in the sense that food and water are 'essential'. And how, for that matter, can any poem be 'essentially New Zealand' in the sense that the kiwi or the whitebait pattie are, in Curnow's phrase, 'peculiarly New Zealand's' ('Attitudes for a New Zealand Poet', iii)? In practice, we found the term 'essential' as essentially constricting as Edmond and Sewell had done.

Moreover, once one poetry anthology has called itself 'essential', what could a second 'essential' anthology do except add the few more 'essential' poems that had been written in the interim? A solution might have been to give the anthology an entirely different title. So, *New Zealand Poems* would have been more accurate, but a touch bland. *Some Rather Good New Zealand Poems the Three of Us Rather Like* would have been honest. But in the end, we decided (after much discussion) to preserve the original title and indicate our difference through a subtitle taken from one of the poems in the collection. The title of Elizabeth Nannestad's poem 'Facing the Empty Page' soon presented itself, offering a phrase that, positively and negatively, embodies the creative process, whether the creator is poet, editor or anthologist — suggesting both courage and difficulty, blankness and making over, desperation and fresh start.

By what additional principles were we guided? Edmond and Sewell began, if not quite at the beginning, with poems by early practitioners such as Jessie Mackay and Blanche Baughan. We in our turn might have plumped for slightly later poets, like R. A. K. Mason, Ursula Bethell, A. R. D. Fairburn, Robin Hyde, Eileen Duggan and the young Allen Curnow, who in their different ways saw themselves establishing a national poetic voice. But including poets from either or both of those periods proved impracticable, unwieldy. Had we been given space for 300 poems and/or been tasked with compiling (yet) another comprehensive anthology of New Zealand poetry, we should no doubt have selected 'essential' poems by those and other earlier poets.

As it was, and because the era marks a watershed in New Zealand society, culture and literature, we chose the 1950s as our starting point. The poets from that time still seem like our immediate predecessors, and we (or our parents) grew up with them and their work. Some, like Curnow and Alistair Te Ariki Campbell, have died relatively recently. The 1950s can, with reservations, be seen to mark the consolidation of the struggle for cultural identity. During that era our foremost literary journal, *Landfall*, grew in importance. It was first published in 1947, and its thirteenth issue, published in 1950, featured poems by Curnow and Baxter. And since the 1950s, and particularly the 1980s, so much that was always present just beneath the ground-cover and gorse of New Zealand poetry has flowered in the work of Alistair Te Ariki Campbell, Hone Tuwhare, Albert Wendt, Robert Sullivan, Tusiata Avia, Hinemoana Baker and others.

So, the 1950s. Our other editorial guidelines? Like our predecessors, we sought to cover the widest possible range in a limited space. For Edmond and Sewell that meant 'No poet is represented by more than four poems'. Like Bill Manhire in his *100 New Zealand Poems* (1993) and its successor, we decided to include one poem by each poet. This of course presented its own challenges. How, after all, can a single poem illustrate the rich diversity of poets such as (the later) Curnow, Baxter, Manhire, Fleur Adcock, Vincent O'Sullivan, Ruth Dallas, C. K. Stead, Elizabeth Smither, Ian Wedde, Lauris Edmond, Kevin Ireland, Michele Leggott . . . ? Of course, it cannot.

We then faced a number of tricky choices. Some poets have such a distinctive voice, such an individual idiolect, that their work is instantly recognisable. Should we choose a poem which demonstrates that voice or choose one which, because it plays against type, is more distinctive? Some poets have 'party pieces' — much-admired and already much-anthologised poems, a number already included in the original *Essential New Zealand Poems*. Should that fact insist on or disqualify the poem's inclusion here?

Our selections, in some cases after much discussion, indicate our decisions. Some poems by well-known poets will, we hope, seem unexpected at first, justified on reflection. Some by lesser-known poets will also surprise and delight.

Finally, in organising the poems, we have rejected classification by subject matter, by publication date, by author chronology or geographical location, and (like Edmond and Sewell) have followed that arrangement which is most 'democratic and easily navigable': poets in alphabetical order.

The pieces you will encounter in this collection are not intended to constitute an encyclopedia of New Zealand poetry of the last 60 years. Rather, from a vast number of poems which, personally or collectively, might equally be regarded as 'essential', we've chosen poems that reflect our subjective preferences. We hope that this anthology, arrived at over many readings, discussions and deliberations by three poets of different ages and experience, will offer a memorable sounding of the depth, diversity and vitality of contemporary New Zealand poetry.

Siobhan Harvey, James Norcliffe and Harry Ricketts
March 2014

THE POEMS

Fleur Adcock

Having Sex with the Dead

How can it be reprehensible?
The looks on their dead faces, as they plunge
into you, your hand circling a column

of one-time flesh and pulsing blood that now
has long been ash and dispersed chemicals.
The half-glimpsed mirror over their shoulders.

This one on the floor of his sitting-room
unexpectedly, one far afternoon;
that one whose house you broke into, climbing

through his bathroom window after a row.
The one who called you a mermaid; the one
who was gay, really, but you both forgot.

They have all forgotten now: forgotten
you and their wives and the other mermaids
who slithered in their beds and took their breath.

Disentangle your fingers from their hair.
Let them float away, like Hylas after
the nymphs dragged him gurgling into the pool.

Johanna Aitchison

Letters from Japanese Kids

Dear Ms Johanna
I very enjoyed your class
I am lonely, but I do my best
I could forget bad feelings

I very enjoyed your class
You are always smiling and talking in a loud voice
I could forget bad feelings
Get a boyfriend and have a happy life

You are always smiling and talking in a loud voice
Sometimes you danced with us so kindly
Get a boyfriend and have a happy life
Sometimes you scolded me, 'Yusuke!'

Sometimes you danced with us so kindly
I don't want to say goodbye but I have to
Sometimes you scolded me, 'Yusuke!'
To tell the truth I need more time to spend with you

I don't want to say goodbye but I have to
I'll always remember that you have a habit to bite your pen
To tell the truth I need more time to spend with you
Is this the end?

I'll always remember that you have a habit to bite your pen
I am lonely, but I do my best
Is this the end
Ms Johanna?

Raewyn Alexander

Old News Curling in the Sun

this wasn't wood after all
or bricks or sensible
scissors shaped a paper dolls' house
the wind had its way
as a choir from hell
get out get out before the thing goes up

standing on the lawn holding hands
sun rising and the house gone

a charcoal line across our island
belted children in the back seat
screeching out windows
insurance paid for the car
we want to live on the water
those of our friends still alive
are at the road with cups and candles

we rip open small towns with a kiss

John Allison

NEAR DEATH EXPERIENCE

At times like these she opens up
his drawer and takes out
his favourite shirt. Unfolding it,
she holds it out in front of her
as though trying it
against him standing there.
And for a long time she is seeing
him again, his eyes,
his quick smile, his chest
against which she laid her head,
his arms enfolding her.
The whole smell and taste of him.
She feels the once familiar
changes, how her skin is gloved
by his touch, her body
an enclosure he turns inside out.
She feels these changes.
She is a tree, standing in a forest
fire. The foliage dissolves,
her limbs are sheathed in flame.
She feels the breath go out of her.
The fire passes, and she is
ash, incandescent, sinking, ash.
The sun is setting. She is
holding the shirt still.
Carefully she folds it, puts it back
again, into his drawer.
Again. It slides shut so easily.

Nick Ascroft

The Status of the Night

The night considers itself & shrugs.
It's passed through here before,
Seen the sunset rattle the city empty,

Leaving only taxis & cats to patrol
Lonely streets. It's seen alcoholics
Reach tired arms longingly towards

The solace of the moon — there,
Sunbathing in the privacy of a clear
Yearlong morning — seen their palms

Fall short of its grip.

It's a calm night, a sleepless widower
Thinks to himself, nice night for a walk.
The night responds in kind, gently

Shadowing the man with a fond darkness —
As the night has done on countless
Occasions to those strollers, bakers,

Drivers, burglars, grievers, the restless
& The resentful who have lent
The night status in their thoughts &

The warmth of consideration.

Tusiata Avia
Wild Dogs Under My Skirt

I want to tattoo my legs.
Not blue or green
but black.

I want to sit opposite the tufuga
and know he means me pain.
I want him to bring out his chisel
and hammer
and strike my thighs
the whole circumference of them
like walking right round the world
like paddling across the whole Pacific
in a log
knowing that once you've pushed off
loaded the dogs on board
there's no looking back now, Bingo.

I want my legs as sharp as dogs' teeth
wild dogs
wild Samoan dogs
the mangy kind that bite strangers.

I want my legs like octopus
black octopus
that catch rats and eat them.

I even want my legs like centipedes
the black ones
that sting and swell for weeks.

And when it's done
I want the tufuga
to sit back and know they're not his
they never were

I want to frighten my lovers
let them sit across from me
and whistle through their teeth.

Stu Bagby

First Dance

Father Doyle and the Sisters decide
a Dance is in order
for Standard Six, a secular
First communion (our parents joke)

to prepare us for life beyond
the Convent. The girls are transformed
from uniforms into beautiful strangers
whose language we boys can hardly

put voice to. I dance.
I dance with Barbara Hackett.
To Perry Como? To Elvis? We dance
to music we will never forget.

*

Forty years later I read of Berlioz
setting off in his sixties to find
the Girl with the Pink Shoes
with whom he once danced when he was twelve.

I don't remember what colour shoes
Barbara Hackett wore when we danced,
or was wearing the next Friday night
when I met her out shopping with her mother.

We blushed, I remember that, and I remember
the way her mother looked at us.
She looked as if the whole wide world
was a very sad place.

Hinemoana Baker

As a Child

Because you have olive skin, she says to me, you should wear black, not white. I was a seer. I haven't seen it yet. I suspect that someone else is driving. The main character: duplicitous, confused, mad. I have no desire to go to America. I write a book with seven chapters, there is a shipwreck in five of them.

If I could be anyone. I search out a plastic bowl from the cupboard, brown with white polka dots you can feel. I fill it with water and, dipping a fine-toothed, orange comb, I wet my long hair from root to tip. Kua noho kūare ahau. I admire the radio. I feel approachable, singing *Twinkle, Twinkle, Little Star*. It is practically swimming out of me.

I lift the portable typewriter onto a wobbly stool on our front steps. A tumbling waterfall of fluorescent orange light around her. Stories of Jehovah, eighty words per minute. After school photographs I say to my mother. What are those funny lights around people? Tihei mauri ora! Tihei māori ora! It makes people envious.

I sit on a step in the sun and type, the whole book in red because the black stripe. Silver, not gold. Dwindling as I get older. Trying to draw with crayon on my arm. I can't get the hang of metres.

Serie Barford

Mongolian Spots

born the night of the comet
my cousin's child had
birthmarks like bruises
with indistinct edges

random imprints of melanin
that dissolved into family lore
before she started school

her birth cry marked a soul
sounding as it flickered
between worlds

that perilous journey
her first migration
was the span of a labourer's hand

Sarah Jane Barnett

When the Sister Walks

The trail is damp so she gathers up the hem
of her habit and scolds her own impatience

as she steps over roots as thick as a boy's wrist. She
is not at her best. When she left he gently pressed

his tattooed palm to the glass barrier. He said,
See ya, Sister. He made a joke — *See you tomorrow.*

He watched her face while she recited from her red-
edged bible. Finally, like a child, his head rested down.

At the lake she makes towards the witness tree,

she holds aside a low-hanging hickory, the seed-nut rattle
exciting a family of yellow-back wasps. They scatter

like bright marbles, afraid or maybe angry
she cries out, *Oh* — *oh* — and stumbles

away from their hide. They are sucked into an undulating
bubble of yellow and vibrate up into the trees.

They haven't hurt her. It is nothing

but on her knees she says, *Oh God, I am thankful
for you.* She wipes a dirty finger across her cheek.

James K. Baxter

Ode to Auckland

Auckland, you great arsehole,
Some things I like about you
Some things I cannot like.

I came to the Art School, carrying the paintings
Of an eighteen-year-old chick.
On the door of one room somebody had written 'Life'
But there was death inside it.

A skeleton hung there by a hook in its skull
Its ribs brown with earth, age, or varnish.
The statue of a Greek god lay on the floor
With his prick and balls knocked off by a chisel.
'Alison,' I said, 'they've buggered the god of death,
They've cut the balls off the god of love.
How can their art survive?'

'Roimata ua, roimata tangata —'
The tears of rain are falling,
Tears of rain, tears of men.

I went to Mass at Newman Hall,
Then visited the Varsity Cafeteria
With six Catholic acquaintances.
One wanted to show me the poems he had written,
One talked about the alternate society,
One wanted to convert the world,
One girl in glasses gave me the glad eye,
Another praised the pentecostal movement,
Another hoed into his plate of cheese and camel turds.

I said, 'Excuse me a minute, there's a Maori friend of mine,
If he doesn't get a place to crash tonight
The cops will pick him up for the four crimes
They dislike most in Auckland,
Not having a job,
Wearing old clothes,
Having long hair,
Above all, for being Maori.
When they shift him to the cells in the meat wagon
The last crime might earn him five punches in the gut.
Could any one of you give him a night's lodging?'

They were extremely sorry.
The bourgeois Christ began to blush on the Cross.
The Holy Spirit squawked and laid an egg.
One had landlord trouble,
One had to swot for exams,
One was already overcrowded,
One didn't know exactly,
One still wanted to show me the poems he had written,
And the last one still silently consumed his plate of camel turds.

I took the Maori lad to Keir Volkerling's place.
He slept on a mattress in the bathroom.
Keir was not a Christian, or a student.
He worked ten hours a day
Digging drains or mixing concrete
To support an average of twenty-five people
Who would otherwise have been in jail
For being out of work,
For wearing an old coat,
For having their hair down to their shoulders,
And above all, for the crime of being Maori.

Christianity has weakened my brain cells, brother,
I haven't got the fortitude of Keir Volkerling.

The Auckland Varsity gives me a pain in the rectum.
I am waiting for the day
When its wedding cake tower goes down in a pile of rubble
From a bomb planted by an intelligent boobhead
Or a not-so-intelligent Varsity radical.

The Auckland Art School gives me a pain in both my testicles.
They don't know the best of Illingworth.
They admire the worst of McCahon.
Why not burn the Art School down
And get some old houses and do a bit of painting
Either with a brush on the ceiling
Or with a brush on a bit of canvas?

I paid a visit to an old friend
Who used to write some good poems.
The door of his office was painted black and yellow,
The colour of the plague flag.

'Peter,' I asked him, 'could you spare me a dollar?'
He looked unhappy.
He was putting on some ceremonial robes
For a meeting of the University Council.
'I'm sorry, man,' I said,
'I didn't mean to interrupt you.'

Outside his office the wind rustled
Dead leaves on the concrete pavement.
I shook hands with an old moss-grown statue
And went barefoot down the road.

Auckland, even when I am well stoned
On a tab of LSD or on Indian grass
You still look to me like an elephant's arsehole
Surrounded with blue-black haemorrhoids.

The sound of the opening and shutting of bankbooks,
The thudding of refrigerator doors,
The ripsaw voices of Glen Eden mothers yelling at their children,
The chugging noise of masturbation from the bedrooms of the bourgeoisie,
The voices of dead teachers droning in dead classrooms,
The TV voice of Mr Muldoon,
The farting noise of the trucks that grind their way down Queen Street
Has drowned forever the song of Tangaroa on a thousand beaches,
The sound of the wind among the green volcanoes,
And the whisper of the human heart.

Boredom is the essence of your death,
I would take a trip to another town
Except that the other towns resemble you exactly.

How can I live in a country where the towns are made like coffins
And the rich are eating the flesh of the poor
Without even knowing it?

O Father Lenin, help us in our great need!
The people seem to enjoy building the pyramids.
Moses would get a mighty cold reception.
They'd kiss the arse of Pharaoh any day of the week

For a pat on the head and a dollar note.
At another time in another place
Among the Ngati-Whatua
When they brought the dead child into the meeting house

She opened her eyes and smiled.

David Beach

Abandoned Novel

It was a dark and stormy day, at least
for the duration of the eclipse. A
huge leaf, resembling a man whose coat was
flapping in the wind, had been proceeding
along a road and the alignment of
heavenly orbs happened to coincide with
the piece of foliage's arrival at
its destination. This was a section
for which it might have been expected to
feel an affinity, abundant trees
concealing any house. The leaf halted
at the gate and then, horrified by the
interruption to photosynthesis
perhaps, began trembling . . . well, like a leaf.

Tony Beyer

Cut Lilac

the dead smell the rain gives
to bunches of cut lilac
in bay windowed living rooms

is another version of the skull
your mouth feels when you kiss
a lover's or a child's clear forehead

but these are impetuous blue
upon the stems that throng
the vase's throat and splay from it

half captive or as free
as wands of light the recent sun
by peering wetly forth outside

has interspersed among them
divining paths like ours in time
that sprawl and gather haltingly

towards the next blind cervix
of the grave the best of us
will shoulder through with joy

Peter Bland

Sorry, I'm a stranger here myself . . .

but I know the seasons
come into it, and wars,
and the shape of a particular landscape
we try to call our own, and the sea
with all that space and distance,
and fellow travellers we meet on the road,
and the dead of course who were here before us
and the millions more who have yet to arrive.

Jenny Bornholdt

VILLANELLE

That summer that wouldn't go
the light was far too bright.
We didn't want to know.

But then we did. Slow,
or fast, the fight?
That summer that wouldn't go.

We couldn't know.
One thing we learned, though, was how might
fails, and that, we didn't want to know.

But then we wanted it all, blow
by crushing blow. After all, it was our right,
that summer that wouldn't go.

And so we sat it out. The glow
of light sinking into a night
we didn't want to know.

But it was the one sure thing. The only
thing we knew. And it was wrong, not right.
That summer that wouldn't go.
That summer we didn't want to know.

Charles Brasch

World Without End

In all weathers? If imagination permit —
If imagination qualifies, then yes, in all.
Do you recall that day when the second war was ending
And from our sterile bureaux
We walked out into the green breath of the Park
Saying, 'Well, nothing more can happen now,
Nothing worse'? And it seemed so that day, that year.
How little we knew. There is always a worse and still worse
And no ending, though each in his turn is broken —
The will crumbled, the heart lost, mind given way,
And to humming hospital or knacker's yard
We are turned over, no longer master of our gates.
The end for each is no ending at all;
World persists, turning with us, in us,
Turned by us in all our weathers,
Intolerable to each, our common country.

Diana Bridge

Jars, Bubble Bowls and Bottle Vases

These are the bowls the rims of which lean
inwards as though they held a secret;

these are the lavender-blue jars and bottle vases,
the small flat dishes of that elect assembly

they call Jun ware. The name gives away nothing.
No clue to the spot implanted deep within,

the splash that wraps around —
but never quite subdues — the opalescent glaze.

*

The more we gaze, the more we want a story . . .
a palace lady passing through the hall once

paused before the flawless body of a bowl
and draped her gauzy shawl over its milky surface.

When it was lifted, islands of peculiar beauty
lay floating on the ocean of its skin.

Now each moon-white vessel bears them.

*

Her tale has yet to run its course. Its tributaries spill,
an archipelago across a plate, a spray of crimson

feathers, a network of capillaries, along the light blue
shoulder of a jar — the mind decides what it sees.

Each molten spot is its own revelation, as though
it were that wound the artist works from.

Each body is transfigured by its markings; each vase
enacts a passage. And so, a splash of purple

tinged with crimson measures the exact shade
of suffering; another maps its shifting shape.

Like badges of maturity, the markings tell us why
a woman cannot look at porcelain with a girl's indifferent eye.

Bub Bridger

A Christmas Wish

I want a Whetton for Christmas!
Either Alan or Gary would do . . .
I'd l-o-o-o-o-ve a Whetton for Christmas
For some frolicsome festival woo
But — they tell me that Gary is married
Still . . . Alan is there to be plucked
And his eyes and his thighs are s-o-o-o-o sexy
And his body just made to be . . . admired.

I hear tell that he is a flanker?
And that sounds such a good thing to be
And his flanks and his shanks and whatever
Could certainly scrum down with me!
I want a Whetton for Christmas!
Big stocking just full to the brim
With a whopping great hunk of a flanker
Clad in nothing more than a grin!

I'd pluck him right out of the stocking
And play ball with him all Christmas Day
Then I'd urge him to score some tries on the floor
And convert them the old-fashioned way . . .
To hell with the difference in ages!
Because age does not matter at all!
O-o-o-o-h-h-hh! If I got a Whetton for Christmas!
Just imagine the rucks . . . and the mauls!

Santa — give me young Alan for Christmas —
And when you ride off on your sleigh
Reflect on the pleasure you've brought me
And heed not his cries of dismay

For I promise he won't be neglected
And before our first game's reached half-time
He'll come to see that there's much more to me
Than an elderly maker of rhyme!

A-a-a-ah-hh . . . but now the World Cup is over
And those Aussies have taken our pride
Well — I want you to know that I'm still all aglow!
That my passion has flowered! Not died!
So . . . I still want a Whetton for Christmas
And still it's that flanker I love
I don't care if the All Black selectors
Want to give him the boot and the shove!

They say he's too old for an All Black
And they say that he's had his time —
I say — What a load of old cobblers!
He's just coming into his prime!
Well — maybe not with a football — but
When it comes to the old one! two! three!
There's nobody else but young Alan
Who could get past the touchline with me!

So — I think I'll kidnap the darling
And carry him off to my lair
Where he can forget all these problems
And just be my big Teddy Bear . . .
He'll be chained to my wrist with a padlock
And he never will get away
He'll be mine! The Angel! Forever!
And Christmas will come every day!

Sarah Broom

DEFROST THE DOG

defrost the dog's dinner he's on raw and must always have tripe
with bones pick up from piano drop get someone to pick up
from soccer drop kick pick up defrost defreeze soak some beans
he's wanting to learn the cello learn to read the bass clef beans
and pick up faster drop the dog's dinner pick up the cello kick
the dog out he's biting the furniture cook the beans up takes
six hours no hard balls in the house please kick and chase and
better use a can we play mums let's play mums you be I'll be no
I want to be no *I* want drop kick get the washing in wash beans
hands no tripe no time for more *tripe* but maybe . . . pick me up?

Amy Brown

Baba Yaga

Lyall Bay is often the scene
of tempests, everything pelted

with salt water, rust spreading
like ill humour. The police

are often patrolling in Lyall Bay.
When the cumulonimbus sit like fat

white cauldrons steaming with cirrus,
look out for the brush strokes —

someone's been sweeping the sky
clean as linoleum after an accident.

Diane Brown

Follow Me If You Will

one a.m. in Quay St
a small black balloon
waits unaccompanied
on the footpath, taking
my heart for a minute

away from the language
of the evening
was it significant
his leaning towards me
and do I want it to be so?

no such doubt exists
for the balloon
things are working out
entirely as expected
it's obvious

by the way it bobs
across the road
jauntily dodging cars
heading straight
for the ferry building

James Brown

NEEDS WORK

You decide to start again. This time, you listen to your parents.
No, you don't. You walk into the forest.
This way. Between these trees.
You like to watch people unobserved.
You like to think about nothing. The space it requires.
The time. You drift along the lines.
When you read, whose voice do you hear?
That sadness you sometimes feel. There? Not there?
Have you ever held on too long? Hold on.
What was your grandmother's maiden name?
You'll have to go back. Between those trees.
You'll have to go on. A reassuring sign.
Here come the margins. Softly. Firmly.
Percentage. Leakage. A nice little earner.
The customary world. According to custom.
People in space and time. The illusion of choice.
The tyranny of choice. Partial information.
Uncertainty. A strain of influences.
Decisions based on networks, hunches, haunches.
Emotions made flesh. Shuddering details.
Good feelings. Bad ideas.
Everything is manipulative.
Soft crotchets. Silence. Actual size.
And always the Big Generals.
Mr Unknown. Mrs Unknowable.
Ms Impossible Spirit. Miss Understanding.
You like a good joke. Does that count?
What about Stan and the Cellphone?
The curve ball? The double curve ball?
Questions. Answers.
Sometimes the answers just come down the phone.

Forget love. You cannot replace it.
Follow love. It will consume your life.
Accept your lot. Don't accept your lot.
Don't join the army. Don't romanticise manual work.
Get a grip. Regain the initiative.
You regain the initiative. But lose focus.
Broad brushstrokes. Depth of field. Negative space.
Nothing you can put your finger on.
You keep on. You could never let things go.
Love's metaphors. Metaphor's warm auditorium.
You slip in at the back. You like to watch people unobserved.
The unwritten rules. Indoor/outdoor flow.
Tongue and groove. Tongue in cheek.
A rustic little charmer. Your own patch of paradise.
Needs work. Needs new shoes. New friends.
Both oars in the water. Haha hoho.
Needs to let go. Start over.
Fresh ideas. A breath of fresh air.
No more apologies. No more nos.
Sorry. You're fresh out of luck.
Missed boats. Loose cannons. The hospital tuck.
Ships that pass in the night.
Darkness. Light.
A flock of seagulls. A flight of steps.
Streamed consciousness. Abandoned sex.
The edge of a crossing. Stillness.
Fullness. Imagination's flossing.
The unlevel spirit. Bless it. Blast it.
Groups and their creations.
Gods. Religions.
Abstractions. Equations.
Particles and waves. Both right and wrong.
An hesitation. Don't worry.
You're the sharpest knife in the poem.
You keep it together. You stay on song.

Cadences. Occasional weather.
Things so much depends upon.
Thought bubbles. A red umbrella. Smiling.
Passing by woods on a snowy evening.
Desire's clarity. A clearing.
Hairs on tan lines. Lines in the sand.
Boundaries as possibilities. A study.
Listen to your heart. Listen to your body.
Baby steps. Sibilance. Minor dings.
The inevitable compromise.
Time flies. Time drags. Time slips.
Time sings.
And then it is time.
Windows. Curtains.

Owen Bullock

ABSTRACTIONS

died again, the ghost slew him
the minefield & ten-tonne weight failed

tomorrow he'll try again not to die
to get out & play, reel & watch the screen

he always knows the time,
complains about *her* in the elongated moment

wishes he'd bought a bow so his son
could play the violin, the passion

waiting, wishes he'd picked a lot of things
differently, a mix of sweets, wishes

he understood his past — such strange words
the abstracts, designed for avoidance

he can't get away from them,
everything is active & especially deliberation

Rachel Bush

She Is Lost

In the ditch, the hay paddock, the Lud River,
Piglet Millie, where are you?
What grief you give my friend
who walks barefoot in the garden
who looks and peers and calls you.
What sadness and loss you leave
to my friend who loved you
who loved your wet snout
who loved your small squeals
who tapped an ice-cream carton
and called, Pig Pig, to make you come
who brought you apples
who loved (a curve fitting her heart)
your solid small rump
your pale rough skin
who misses you and mourns you
who calls out and cries for you.
Now the pig pen she made is a vacancy
and the ice-cream container, a reproach
and all the calls of my friend are unanswered.

Kate Camp
Personal Effects

I went to the Kilbirnie Watchtower to pick up your personal
effects from a policeman with your name.
The faint sun made me sweat a little in the car
in my cream rabbit-fur jacket you've never seen.
The policeman was absent so a woman not in uniform
gave me the brown envelope, the size of a foot,
and I held it against my stomach, in the fur,
as I walked back out to the car.

And there wasn't much in it:
a wallet, and $3.15 in change, and a white cigarette lighter.
It was all there, as they'd promised, and the lighter was still going strong,
good as new, and the wallet from Kingston Leather was soft
and moulded like someone made a cast of your pocket,
and there were cards in there, a tiny stack of cards, so I laid
them out in a line on the table and didn't really try to divine
anything from them.

There was a student ID, community services card and a ten-trip
bus ticket, three sections, with one clip left on it.
There were copy cards, national and city library cards
and phone cards and one card read *IRIDOLOGY:*
EYES SHOW OUR ENTIRE BODY'S HEALTH.
And I looked to see which sector of the iris denoted irony
and which despair but the closest I could find was *Reality Coping*
and *Chest Cavity,* and then, just as I was about to put the cards away,
I saw the little key that showed the location of the heart —
according to iridology — right in close to the pupil.

Alistair Te Ariki Campbell
Te Rauparaha in Old Age

You would not have recognised him —
    the old man throwing bits of sticks
        into the campfire and poking it,
and chuckling while he reminisced
    about the old days when his blood
        ran like quicksilver
through his veins. He sat hunched
    over the fire, a blanket
        round his shoulders, with no
regrets and as free of remorse
    as a young child, his chief
        enemy now the cold that nipped
his toes and caused his bones
    to ache. 'Yes, the Wairau —
        bad trouble that, made worse
by the insolence and stupidity of
    the Pakeha. I didn't want bloodshed,
        but what could I do? Rangihaeata's
woman had been shot, and it was
    right that he should ask for *utu* —
        a life for a life — and that
would have been enough, honour
    would have been satisfied,
        but the Pakeha wanted . . .
I don't know what the Pakeha wanted.
    Their ways even today
        are a mystery to me.
More shots were fired, and the Pakeha
    were cut down, one after the other —
        none was spared. A lot of scores
were settled that day. Some Pakeha

hid themselves in the scrub
and were flushed out by dogs.
It wasn't good to see young braves
whooping and carrying on like children
as they ran after them.
War is not a game, but a serious matter —
a testing time for both the slayer
and the slain. The musket
changed all that of course: the victor
no longer loves the man he kills
nor is he loved in return . . .
All that was long ago, *e hoa*.
I am tired and glad enough
to be sitting by this fire
drinking hot tea and rum,
under a moon with the cold
unblinking stare of a god.'

Meg Campbell

My Countrywoman

She is the Kiwi, the Dodo bird
of the South Seas, weak-eyed,
with heavy legs and arse
and beak that doubles as a weapon —
pecking sharpens her mind.
Violent and amiable, both, she is
often seen at shopping centres
flanked by kids and elderly mother.
Sometimes she is seen in the undergrowth
of jumble sales or church bazaar,
pressing to the front, her money
extended to buy the tastiest cake.
In the bedroom, at night, she sports
tiny wings — the curious remnant
of her long-lost flight.

Gordon Challis

Poem for Magda

When I am fit to speak of love the words will come
as easily as wheat puts forth its ample grain
or sunlight skips bright stones across a river.
My tongue thus far is husked and makes harsh sound
and shall not sing until I hear the growth of grain,
until I hear your name in all things blessed forever.

When I am fit to speak of love you may be past
your crest of youthful movement and your grace of line.
It will be late to praise you, late to flatter
myself by implication, finder of your eyes.
And there will be no need to find new ways
to ask or tell each other what's the matter.

When I am fit to speak of love will be a day
of neither signs nor revelation. It might occur
some time when sleeping at my side I'll feel you cry
and wake to hands that make your dream not true,
some moment when you're ironing or touch your hair —
simple and warm as clothes fresh-folded on a chair.

Janet Charman

INVIGILATOR

students flood
the assembly hall
till
it's a think tank
where curved green backs
and agitated hands
navigate the exam

no one can help them

i'm a wharf post in the back
wash

hear a pin drop
in the dense wet
light of
the assessment

all together now
fish
rise from the deep
compose with the miraculous force of your schooling

in the jelly sway of the kelp forest
the names glitter
and vanish

Geoff Cochrane

The Last of Bashō

i

Bashō writes of the purple wine he likes.
Of the barman's slim syringe and black nail-polish.
Of the ten-dollar note burning in the ashtray.
Of the silver airship moored above the pines,
the tethered airship going nowhere slowly.

ii

The snide sirens dive and the rain catches fire,
but what of the Bengal engine's mango afterglow?

iii

Bashō alone and walking some high path.
Bashō alone and climbing the concrete steps to heaven,
a flask of gin in his satchel.
A flask of gin and a spring roll gone cold.

Glenn Colquhoun

To the girl who stood beside me at the checkout counter of Whitcoulls bookstore in Hamilton on Tuesday

For ten seconds I fell
in love with you.

The first second we met.

You were buying recipes.

The second second we turned,
Taking pieces of each other out of our eyes.

The third second we held each other gently.
Your skin was a small kitten playing with a curtain.

The fourth second we kissed.

Front gates clicked against our fence.

In the fifth second we married.
Your dress was made of nikau palm.

The sixth second we built a house beside a lake

It was never tidy and the grass was up to our knees.

The seventh second we argued:

About toothpaste and poetry
and who would put out the rubbish.

The eighth second we grew fat and happy
and laid on the ground after eating.

Your stomach wriggled with a round child.

In the ninth second we were old in the same garden
of the same house by the same lake in the same love.

The tenth second we said goodbye.

Your hand slipped away from mine but
seemed to me like something I could feel.

We passed again beside each other without turning

As though we had somehow only met at the checkout
counter of Whitcoulls bookstore in Hamilton
on a faintly blue September Tuesday.

Kay McKenzie Cooke

Feeding the Dogs

Follow
the torch's twitch
picking out dead thistles,
wooden railings.
Where the ground shines,
bare, snarled
by the roots
of trees, the dogs bark,
rattle chains that drag
over old bones.
Throw them the meat,
pale traces of fat clinging
to the wool of your gloves.

Hear the crush of bones,
the night closing in
the cry of two birds
flying out over rocks.
See ticking stars
in a blind sky.
Softer than light,
darkness leans in
— so close, so cold,
its breath is all
you can breathe.

Allen Curnow

You Will Know When You Get There

Nobody comes up from the sea as late as this
in the day and the season, and nobody else goes down

the last steep kilometre, wet-metalled where
a shower passed shredding the light which keeps

pouring out of its tank in the sky, through summits,
trees, vapours thickening and thinning. Too

credibly by half celestial, the dammed
reservoir up there keeps emptying while the light lasts

over the sea, where it 'gathers the gold against
it'. The light is bits of crushed rock randomly

glinting underfoot, wetted by the short
shower, and down you go and so in its way does

the sun which gets there first. Boys, two of them,
turn campfirelit faces, a hesitancy to speak

is a hesitancy of the earth rolling back and away
behind this man going down to the sea with a bag

to pick mussels, having an arrangement with the tide,
the ocean to be shallowed three point seven metres,

one hour's light to be left, and there's the excrescent
moon sponging off the last of it. A door

slams, a heavy wave, a door, the sea-floor shudders.
Down you go alone, so late, into the surge-black fissure.

Ruth Dallas

Photographs of Pioneer Women

You can see from their faces
Life was not funny,
The streets, when there were streets,
Tugging at axles,
The settlement ramshackle as a stack of cards.
And where there were no streets, and no houses,
Save their own roof of calico or thatch,
The cows coming morning and afternoon
From the end-of-world swamp,
Udders cemented with mud.

There is nothing to equal pioneering labour
For wrenching a woman out of shape,
Like an old willow, uprooted, thickening.
See their strong arms, their shoulders broadened
By the rhythmical swing of the axe, or humped
Under loads they donkeyed on their backs.
Some of them found time to be photographed,
With bearded husband, and twelve or thirteen children,
Looking shocked, but relentless,
After first starching the frills in their caps.

Lynn Davidson

Cape Gooseberries

In a canopy
over the curves
of the hose
the Cape gooseberry plant
suspends its Chinese lanterns.
The fluted cases transparent
as peeled skin;
inside, the orange centre
glows. Beside the house
it glows, as though it were
candle light. It attends to beauty.
Inside the power bill clamours
for attention, noisier
than the t.v., noisier
than the children. If
I pay it all today we could
eat Cape gooseberries for dinner,
rolling the orange orbs
on our tongues, glimpsing
their small light
between our teeth.

Stephanie de Montalk
Concrete

In the weeks before he laid the path
to the front door
and put in steps
from the side entrance to the basement

he went to the library and borrowed a manual
sat weekends at a website
and talked at length in his lunch hour
with others
who had made the journey before him.

'Concrete's a male thing,' he said
'we appreciate the details of durable materials
the comparative benefits of embedded metals

and the step-by-step techniques
by which reinforced steel
in the form of rods, bars, or wires
can be stretched and retracted
to predetermined limits

better than you do

blokes can relate to it
we have a sense of it

there's a lot more to concrete
than the bonding
of sand and water
with stone and cement

there's a history of structural form to consider
think of the lighthouse
after oil lamps, torches, and antiquity

I'm talking about isolated rocks
exposure to the sea
strength without mass

a slender tower
a spiral base
and a design which allows a cylinder
to be set in the sea

think of the way it sets
around the tautly drawn wire
in the curves
and reinforced spans
of the world's major bridges

think of the classical example
of the Colosseum
iron clamps in its joints
enclosed on all sides

and the small volume of poems
around 80 AD
which celebrated its construction.
There are correlations,' he murmured

‘between concrete
cubism
and the visual construction of verse

you can make a poem
out of concrete items
like iron
or eggshells

in the case of rain
you can let the letters fall in long slanting lines
consider e.e. cummings
famous for his typographical eccentricities

or the visually innovative man
in his workshop

making goddesses for the garden
and gnomes
with knives in their backs
he is doing a similarly tangible thing
I’m told that his aliens
Mexicans
and tyre-marked opossums
are popular

that people have been known
to write the names of their pets
on the necks of the replicas
he makes for them

but perhaps I’m straying nearer to philosophy here —
concrete as distinct from abstract
it’s an interesting area —

concrete as real life
concrete as a bird
balanced with precision
on the uppermost branch of a tree

as a boy riding a skateboard

as existential experience

as concrete as rigid paving

this could mean we are talking
vegetation clearing
earthmoving
graders and bulldozers

the size and weight of traffic using the highway

the possibility
of underground streams

a system by which we can carry rainwater
to shallow gutters
at the edge of the shoulder

and the likelihood of erosion
if the steps are cut
into the wrong sort of hillside

in which case
we'll need a building code
for the slope

and a plan of action
should ground water drain
down the back of the section

and the earth start to slip
in the absence
of a retaining wall.

Look at this diagram —
sub-base
compaction
and a layer of concrete —

it raises questions of
shrinkage
temperature control
and warping of the slab
due to moisture variations
between top and bottom

and means that
on a summer's day

hosing of the garden
or lawn
on either side of the pathway

or more particularly
the steps

could lead to
cracking
crumbling

and the undignified sight
of concrete
losing its grip on the hillside.'

*

His path to the front door
was an unqualified success.

Later, he built the steps
to the basement

and every one of them
was unique.

John Dickson
SLEEPER

on my birthday, the Angel had questions
your performance to date, your career path.
And when he'd finished, I said, Angel
we've been through all this before.
I have everything I need, a desk, a chair
paper and pens. And though I sometimes
hear voices murmuring in the next room
like old people who have lost their past
it's no problem; there's no discrepancy
between what's said and what I hear.
And the view is simply splendid.
Every night, after I close the blinds
the bush splits open the wooden houses
and plank by plank takes them back;
and every morning, the houses are there again
waiting for you to raise the dead.
As for my work, it's obvious to me
you haven't read the job description
you yourself wrote. Must I remind you?
And since you asked, I know nothing now
about life in history, whether it goes round
and round in a great returning circle
(better rise above it friend
otherwise you will drop right through)
or whether like some vast machine
it moves towards a predetermined end
(better join it friend, otherwise
you will get left behind), for all I know
maybe everything that happens
happened in a present time so vast
it's the size of the universe and twice as fast

walk past a Gallipoli veteran
and Troy burns once more, a storm
may be blowing from paradise
piling wreckage upon wreckage
before your feet, and with such force
you can never close your wings
Thermopylae, Rwanda, My Lae
Yellow Tiger, Hitler, Pol Pot
I know nothing about such things
or what could be done for human good
but if I've heard you right, I should go back
and help bring meaning to their carnage.
Angel, who are you kidding?
I'm not an unsuspecting tenor from Oklahoma
singing, Oh what a beautiful morning.
When I wake in my room, I'm nothing
but a shadow on a wooden wall
a minor bureaucrat amongst the angelic orders.
I write reports. I follow instructions
here and there correcting a comma.
I've no need to change eternity
for a place full of colour and life
but where word and thing are not the same.
Leave them to it, they have your gift
the structural unreliability of freedom.
And as for having answers.
Such debauchery of the soul!
Mountains are mountains, rivers are rivers
and my face is just my face.
Your choice, he said, and I went back
to my small room and fell fast
into a deep and wakeful sleep

Emily Dobson
from A Box of Bees

Sometimes barefoot, I crossed
the warm road to the honey factory,

my young body a smudge of heat
in the darkening evening, careful of dead bees —

which can still sting — to make candles
alone in the empty factory. I flirted

with the odd beekeeper
returning from pollination.

Then I went back over the road
through the quiet night

to Nanna and Grandad's house,
where I boarded, and climbed into bed.

Through my window: Nanna's grapevines,
honey trucks, the lights of Hastings and stars.

Lauris Edmond

Late Song

It's a still morning, quiet and cloudy
the kind of grey day I like best;
they'll be here soon, the little kids first,
creeping up to try and frighten me,
then the tall young men, the slim boy
with the marvellous smile, the dark girl
subtle and secret; and the others,
the parents, my children, my friends —

and I think: these truly are my weather
my grey mornings and my rain at night,
my sparkling afternoons and my birdcall at daylight;
they are my game of hide and seek, my song
that flies from a high window. They are
my dragonflies dancing on silver water.

Without them I cannot move forward, I am
a broken signpost, a train fetched up on
a small siding, a dry voice buzzing in the ears;
for they are also my blunders
and my forgiveness for blundering,
my road to the stars and my seagrass chair
in the sun. They fly where I cannot follow

and I — I am their branch, their tree.
My song is of the generations, it echoes
the old dialogue of the years; it is the tribal
chorus that no one may sing alone.

Murray Edmond
The Cold War

The cold war was at home
and it also filled the whole earth
a fallout shelter in the backyard
a Russian car you did not want

undiscussability and non-initiation
its apostles had spread out through the world
in a religious kind of movement
the name of Patrice Lumumba was pure language power

the invocation of the lost and future world
became our daily bread
you are feeding the chickens
with your little friend a tiny white-skinned boy in knickers

your *babcia* watches
the cold war was always going to last forever
it had no choice and neither did we
it was a kind of character or relative

your grandfather holds the reins of the horse
the horse is coming into the picture from the right
the Russian car is in the background
how much worse off you were

we loved the cold war like we loved ice cream
it gave us peace silence time to resent
gift-wrapped and ticking it passed from hand to hand
content to keep its content hidden in a form

David Eggleton

Titirangi Considered as Wearable Art

Fringe of heaven, half-clad in glad rags
of mist embroidered with drizzle,
your weatherboarded, brick-veneered,
rubber-wheeled, possum-furred build-up
extends from roadways and bike trails,
from mown verges, and from ponga arcades
that, mud-stepped, down gullies parade
as if to salute shops along your main drag.

Bush suburb, spiralling, a fern provider,
you're decorated by wasps' paper nests,
and by pole-houses that want to flap out,
like wind-cradled box kites pulled taut,
while birds scatter-wheel to flutter
over canopies of trees rooted in legends
dug from the skull of the moa, and
hymned in the rasp of the cicada.

Silver sequins tremble on leaf-weave
of shawl draping your shadowy ranges,
and rolling to the lace of Tangaroa's sea.
Tangata whenua carved Tane from kauri;
sawmill blades set the god free to change;
but he crumbled among moth grubs, breathing
out showers of sawdust in a kind of bleeding
to stain subdivisions that no longer believed.

Titirangi, your sunset blazes in amber resin,
your huia feathers gleam in museum gloom.

Ferns lose themselves; darkness finds coast;
a blurred kingfisher flees from a fence-post.
Eel-ladders descend to the world's womb:
stacked and storied trenches of Hine-nui-te-po,
her kiln-like cave, from where shapes grow,
and the first frond of morning uncurls green.

Riemke Ensing

Hokianga Love Song

In the hollowed trunk of the puriri tree
wild bees have made honey. They hum
songs in the vault of shining leaves and drink
from flowers sensuous in the green dark.
We too have had our fill of nectar and watch
light crochet moving patterns of shade
through branches making wide verandahs. We lie
remembering how houses grew from local timbers
(kauri mostly, *Agathis australis*, with totara
for blocks) and the wind blew from up harbour
light as your encircling arms in this summer grass
tousled blond by sun licking its warm tongue
across our bodies salt with the sea where the taniwha
lives behind rocks wreathed in swirls of kelp. We
follow the tumbling drift of curves coming and going
and coming together again as lovers on tides undisturbed
by gulls, and in that turbulence our bodies are solemn
as hills that shape with the burden of stories older
than ancient weeping waiata and the naming of past
under the light blue winking leaves of sky.

Rangi Faith

Advice to a Colonial Artist

The moa hunter should be sketched
with a fine ink and brush —
that way he should slip
into the landscape from the margin —
he should wash over us
& not ungently so,
for he too will leave
the mark of the hunter
in his wake.

The man from England
has his legacy sealed in wax;
his beginnings are gilt-edged —
he sweeps boldly across the canvas
his ambitions fired in red:

here, the blue slash of the plough,
there, the crimson slice of the harpoon,
& here the black smear of the factory
& the gun.

Leave the whites until last
so that the bones of the people
show through.

And who shall sign
for this masterpiece?

Fiona Farrell

Fairytale

for Jane and Antoinette

There were two sisters in the story.
Remember? One dark, one fair. And a
bear who came in to lie by the fire.
So they learned early that appearances
deceive and that it's wise to be polite
to hags and goblins. Kiss the frogs.
You just can't tell in forests where
light flickers and reality can change
in seconds. And one night the dark
sister walked out and met death who
wasn't old as they expected: dim and
toothless, dwindling to decay but a
young man riding who gathered her up
wild into the storm. And the fair one
seeks her still in daffodils and all
bright vivid things because she knows
that in this forest shapes shift, fit on
new skins, but nothing vanishes
completely. The right words said with
love can spring a sudden transformation.

So she lives. We hope happily.
And we hope ever after.

Cliff Fell

Alive

At the next post
he sees the broken strands of wire
flapping free. He knows
the short is there —
can hear its click-click
like a gorse-pod in the sun.
He kneels on the damp ground,
groping for fallen staples
in the long uneaten grass,
and waiting to feel his fingers draw the current,
the shock howling up his arm —
a voice to say he's alive on the earth
breathing the sweet air,
walking the paddocks from one gate to another.
He sees the world down there:
a bee feeds in the pink of clover flowers,
brimstone-blue moths flutter up,
shedding grass-seed from their wings
and somewhere beyond the manuka
the creek makes a low whicker
as though the soul of the valley was a horse.

Jan FitzGerald

Cows Crossing

Cows slow the car to an indolent amble,
surround us with the pink mammary smell
of themselves.
Don't mind us, they say, and we won't mind you
as long as you fall in behind,
learn how to cow-walk,
watch the marking of non-time
with our metronomic tails . . .
And what are you doing in that glass cage, anyway?
A bony head looms alongside
turning a neck a child would love to swing from,
a neck of teddy bear hair and old hay.
Her breath mists the window,
eyelashes come down
like slow camera shutters.
Never mind, never mind, it takes all sorts . . .
Her big, sassy hips sway past.
Move on, move on . . .
She is carrying a peach balloon to a party
that happened long ago.
Never mind, never mind . . .

Joan Fleming

Armchair Talking to the Window

You are glassy and thin and bluish. Your one role in life is to appear as invisible as possible.

All day, *you* sit there empty. And all evening, you're weighted down with people's behinds. You were once a tree and an animal, and now you're just a servant to the end-of-day.

You've killed three birds already this year, and countless flies. Your false airiness is cunning.

You're sagging a little in the middle, old man. And your arms are cracking.

Have you ever had someone fall asleep in your arms? Have you ever been sighed in? Cried in?

My sisters are cold, hard, diamonds in the sky. We shine together every night.

I'll go the way my father went. I'm happy to die an old chair's death.

My next incarnation will be as the unbreakable air.

Janet Frame

The Place

The place where the floured hens
sat laying their breakfast eggs,
frying their bacon-coloured combs in the sun
is gone.

You know the place —
in the hawthorn hedge
by the wattle tree
by the railway line.

I do not remember these things
— they remember me,
not as child or woman but as their last excuse
to stay, not wholly to die.

Janis Freegard
SAPPHIRE

I was fifteen and working in a department store in my school holidays.
  I would see her on the street sometimes, her hair long enough
  to touch the backs of her knees; she must have been growing it
  her whole life. Hair like sunshine, fine and light, falling to earth.

All I could think of was gazelles.
  She was a delicate antelope in high heels. Her hair swung as she walked.
  A woman at work whispered that she was a prostitute.

I followed her the length of Queen Street one Friday night.
  She wore a sleeveless dress of sapphire blue. I kept a few metres behind
  her. Whenever she turned her head, I faked an interest in the nearest shop
  window. She looked as though nothing could touch her.

I wanted to stop her in the street and ask her what sex was.
  I wanted to know if she could choose them, the men,
  or if she had to sleep with anyone who wanted her.

I thought that, if I were rich enough, I'd buy some of her time.
  I'd rent an evening with her knee-length hair. I imagined going into a room
  that smelt of Opium perfume. The sheets on the bed would glow like
  sapphires. She would reach for my hand.

The sun would come, then, hammering through the window, lifting us up.
  And the sapphire sheets would twist themselves through her hair to make a
  road to the sky. We'd be gazelles together.

  Cantering upwards.
  Rising into the light.

Anne French

The Lady Fishermen

Imagine Jane Austen in thigh waders perfecting
her rolling cast, or Miss Elizabeth Barrett
dashing off to the bush for a weekend's
pig-shooting. Mrs Melville perhaps, at the helm
for the two a.m. watch while Herman snatched
some sleep? Ludicrous. There's no tradition.
We'll just have to improvise (with improvements).

Take yesterday, for instance, drift fishing
in the dinghy off Rakino, five snapper in an hour.
Hauled up from thirty feet they screeched
as their swim bladders burst. Dead on arrival
in the bucket. And tonight I performed the graceful
act in my civilized kitchen: a sharp knife turning
one fish into two fillets and a pile of odds and ends.

Almost taken in by it, the poetry of catching
dinner, the magic of flesh turning white in the pan,
golden in its jacket of crumbs, decorated with a salad
of tomatoes and red onions as lurid as a paperback.
You might prescribe it as a known antidote to *branlement*
littéraire (that common affliction). Emily, pulling
steadily on the oars; Janet, slicing up the mullet bait.

Rhian Gallagher

Salt Water Creek

What did I ask you, water of no-going,
sluggish as a trough, forsaken
grey-song trundling round the town's back?

Beyond you roads lay, the sea
decked with harbour, freighters from Russia
leashed to the port.

I'd run through paddocks
on the scent of a climate change,
skirting the home radar, five miles out.

I was a cargo,
ready to weigh on a good tide.
Or be swept by the rails
with my ear to the pulse, tick-tack of journey
inside the snake of a train.

You were my first border, channel to be crossed,
like all water you had no ties.
I looked into the halt of you, torpid
and speechless, while the reeds and the wind
made sad-worded songs.

The wavering found me
on the greasy mud of your side,
caught in a slip between worlds
where the woollen mill cast its dyes
and the salt marsh oozed.

A heron broke its own stillness,
wings turning to smoke as it rose.
The man in the petrol station called home.

I stalled among the day weeds, dock and thistle,
under a cloud, awaiting my father
with all that the water said, a water
of no ilk, paler than darkness.

Denis Glover

Towards Banks Peninsula

PERAKI

Anywhere you farm is the sound
Of the surge and surround of the sea.
Valley and gully re-echo the roar
Of the open wound running raw,
The mystery and maw of the sea.

By the loom of the reef
Or a tide-hidden shoulder of land
In a wind cloud-barred or teasing,
A yacht is a leaf.

But off in the east the boat sings
Before thunders of sunrise are born
In the crisp, wet-running dawn
Where undulous mountains stand
Nebulously for land.

Sailing under the pock-marked wall
Known only to the gull
The yacht comes porpoise-happy from the blue,
Noses past crayfish caves
To gruff-sharp waves
On the terminal beach steep-to.

High on the beach is a whalebone arch
Propped up there long ago
Through whose emptiness we watch
Unmovingly Whale Rock surface and blow.

Paula Green

Two Minutes Westward

We take ourselves like mountain goats up the muddy
track, cloud before rock, rock before flax because
in the stillness we find the noise of an ocean
sinking roots sunk fierce
into how to be westward.
Westcoast skin. Westcoast blood. Westcoast bone.
Stepping into this sweet cyclone of silence
we are pinned to the inlet cool and spare
like a roving eye
disappearing and feeding on heavenly wings
halfway to paradise
with a divine map for romance
those perspiring sonnets and me doubled back
laughing like death.
This is high and on the edge
vertigo looping the Te Henga cliff tops
behind us a flower might blossom
a musical note might flare
but one thing's for sure
here on cold mornings
here where love is snacking
the risk of heights punctuates
a risk we take
our heartbeats startled at the startled kereru.
A word for his skin
a word for his bone
a word for his blood
then memory steadies the erring waterfall
the white plume of the heron all dried up.

Still I keep the ancient preserve of kauri
stuck in my guts
some kind of brace
because I will hurl
all the old figures over the edge
in one foul swoop
down there into the seething
steaming black sanded
heart of the west coast sea.
Holding his hand at midnight
beneath the starry sky
I will try and let Ulysses loose
and Virgil's honey-tongued
ritorniamo nel chiaro mondo?
Vediamo le cose belle
che porta il cielo?
Holding his hand at midnight and kissing those
amber lips here in the light belief
that a word will dig the pit
for the featherweight myth.
Turn your head my dearest to the left
stand still and hear the droning brook
or the otherwhere hum of the bee.
Still. Stand still. Turn your ear to the right
and hear the wind rubbing across the track
a pocket of nectar and linseed oil
pressing against my spine.
Would we take a boat home
across the wild comfort?

David Gregory

THE CRUISE

Once round the deck
once round the chipped
rim of the Pacific
we perform for the natives
towing in our jaded sunsets
for another fertility dance
like groping
for a light switch
only to realise you
should have stayed
in the dark
where the ship
scatters its postcards
in the inky sea
the finely ground night
with its mica stars
sticks in your throat
and the moon
heavily made up
joins you at the rail.

Bernadette Hall
The Lay Sister

The lay sister slides her hands
through holy water. Chops
onions, carrots, celery

in that order. Splits
blocks of wattle. Her hands
are fat on the axe handle.

'Good God,' says the Bishop,
slipping another smoke ring
round the crystalline throat

of the Portuguese sherry
decanter. 'That woman
would knock you down as good

as look at you!' The lay sister
is as rough as guts, speaks
Irish rather than English,

sleeps through the mission,
eats by herself in the kitchen.
Sometimes however

they do let her answer
the door and it's 'Excuse me,
Reverend Mother, there's

a piano in the parlour'
(that's the given code word
for a man) and she not able

to keep herself from laughing
then, imagining knocking
a fine old tune out of him.

Michael Harlow

And, Yes

Sometimes your touch
love's homecoming is
Not to put too fine a call
on what heart knows
despite head's long
success in all silly else;
that is, by 'all flowers'
and these candles,
love's invitations you
light up a parcel of dark,
the way your breasts
wear sunlight: the heart
has reasons reason
cannot know. The green
wild call of spring
that waits over the hill,
and here in love's bed
wants me you to kiss
and all our trulys touch.
And that is the story
about yes: never trust
a god who does not dance.

Siobhan Harvey

Tooth

Today, you're twelve teeth old,
and we fossick for shells,
starfish, pipi and paua

until the tide goes out
when we wave goodbye
to yachts moored in the marina.

At home, you float
across polished floors
until you keel over.

Your jaw leaves an alveolus
in the matai deep enough
for a teardrop's caress.

As I stroke you,
your eyes collect water;
your gums are an ocean of blood.

But only when you're sleeping,
do I discover a tooth
anchored to blue woollen blanket.

Suddenly, you're eleven teeth old
and have grown, like Lazarus,
younger beneath moonlight.

White and hull-shaped,
tooth's a boat,
isolated by low tide.

In the morning,
I'll show you how it can rest
safely upon its starboard.

Dinah Hawken

The Tug of War

Is a scene that rises in her mind. A long line of men, say 100,
facing north, holding a long rope. A long line of women, say 110,
facing south, facing the men, holding the same long rope.
They are all dressed in late 19th century clothes, standing ready
on the shore-line of a long New Zealand beach. A long line
of surf is breaking.
The rope is clearly visible in the gap
where the first man faces the first woman. Here the starter also
stands. He is shouting into a megaphone:
'Take the strain — get ready — go!' So the tug
of war begins. Equal weight and equal strength on each
side. Centuries of struggle are rising
in the blood of each man and each woman and at the exact
moment that they judge the men to be at the height
of their physical and mental power, the women
let the rope go.

They love to let go and they love to get going:
they get themselves going and they let themselves go.
They let love go and they get love going:
they get others going and they let others go.
They let life go and they get life going,
they live to give love and they love to let live.

Helen Heath

Ripple

The floor has a ripple
in it, which is funny
because the carpet is blue
like the sea and the baby
is pulling and chewing
on my nipple so hard
that it bleeds
and her little legs kick-
kick me, her hands find
my hair and pull hard
and there's a roaring
in my ears that might
be the sea and they ask
me if I'm blue and
I say I just need
some sleep then everything
will be all right but now
the floor has a ripple in it.

Jeffrey Paparoa Holman

from THE LATE GREAT BLACKBALL BRIDGE SONNETS

XXIII

In the house of my body I carry that river.
In the depths of my being I'm water. My

body's the home of a wandering miner
too old to go down and too tired to go on.

When I stand on the world and look over
what's living, what's left, I'm the bridge

to the past and the road still unfolding.
Wheels and water, tracks and steam, all

the footprints beside the river, thousands
of hours spent double in blackness, a light

on my head to remind me I'm human. In
the shape of my bones I'm an NZR sleeper

and when my last shift comes, my Dog Watch
boys, lay me like coal by the sea at Karoro.

Ingrid Horrocks

Light Between Houses

Wellington, May
for T

Has this always been my favourite time
of day, when orange street lamps come on
all at once between houses,
or is it that this year as winter deepens
and night drops ever earlier over the city,
I know you are walking
towards me, past tulip beds, heavy
magnolia trees, crossing roads on the
painted stripes of zebras' backs?

People move in and out of the dairy on the corner
where last night we bought wood for the first
fire of the year. There in the brightness
as we talked back and forth, forth and back
each word seeming to come from a depth
in our bodies; we hardly touched before
I pushed against you and tasted your skin.

Dark now, hillsides patterned by lights
from kitchen windows. Soon you will turn
the last bend. Soon you will be here,
silent or singing, empty-handed
or with a warm loaf of bread.
How will you look when I see you,
and you see me? There are only lights now
and we are both outside. Somewhere,
slowly, some kind of moon must be rising.

John Horrocks

Weather Report — Fine

Jan 17, 1901: Fine warm feel of thunders clear evening
Jan 18, 1901: Fine warm cloudy a heavy wind NW
Jan 19, 1901: Fine but cloudy not so warm heavy weather
Jan 20, 1901: Fine warm slight rain
Jan 21, 1901: Fine hot rain about 6 for a short time. Fine evening
Jan 22, 1901: Fine and very warm

It's the weather that tells me,
reading your diary, this is the same place.
Your words leave prints like isobars
marking the touch of rain and sun.

A hundred years have changed nothing.
I hope you got your lambs shorn
before the black sou-wester showed,
driving all the way from Antarctica.

Fine rain would have been welcome.
Rain not so sharp you had to put
wet lambs back in the draughty shed,
wind blowing through the noisy slats.

That's when children, like ours, lay
on the hot stones by the pool, the one
where the Kiriwhakapapa turns
towards the Waipoua and the sea.

The air would thicken, heavy
and warm with thunder, drenched
with the feeling of fine summers,
indifferent to all forecasts of winter.

David Howard

A Simple Chronology

1) 517 St Asaph Street (1966)

Check blankets were best:
a caress was useless, you had to haul
until they followed the body's
folds. *Made in Mosgiel*
meant warmer than Lucifer —
not that he was from around here.

On the sill were jam jars of flowers,
last spring's water
darker than any petal. A drunk
sobered by the love of some girl
who intoxicated others, you snuggled
under as if this was your earth.

2) School Sports (1972)

The girls always
avoiding us.
One body, one
more walking off
across scorched grass,
sucking hard on
answers. Laughter
marking the air

the way hunger
swells the bell —
as a promise

gone rotten. Not
wanting to be
beyond 'beyond'.

3) Lyttelton (1984)

Curling over the mantel
a postcard of an anchor
rather than an anchor, although
they're not going anywhere
so what's the difference? He
flicks a grin made of
licorice Lagavulin and perhaps
as that anchor in her drags.

4) Marshland Road (1992)

Scrubbing front steps
mothers consider the shopping centre
opposite: it's not as if there's a lot
else. Twelve bloody months
the hammering and then
Opening Specials

spilling from trolleys that rattle
asymmetrically west. Seeing
red as their men collect
kegs in Escorts, judder-
bar past the present tense
where a stop sign means you're gone, mate.

5) Port Chalmers (2003)

That calendar cottage meant rent
overdue. However picturesque,
hawthorn hurt your hands

whether they were a labourer's
or a lover's: the blood
dropped regardless. Eventually

'the best of both worlds'
reduced to a view of the moon
peering over a long drop;

to Peter Kaan, Port Chalmers' fruiterer
who died three weeks after
retiring: 'I'm going to pack up

and clear off.' *And.*

[30.9–8.10.2004]

Keri Hulme

Waiting on the Laughing Owl

It is a good night for watching
steady moon/lake mirroring light
stern trees rearing skyward
(hazy) and backing limestone cliffs
ripe with little crevices and holes wherein
might hide the last laughing owl
— hear old authors/longdead listeners talk back from books:
'a bray like a jackass'
'a kicked dog, a whipped pup'
'a scream to raise
horripilation'
(a right conjurer that last one) —
anyway we are huddled under a blanket
admiring the surround
not cold as the fire reaches for the moon
whispering, taking a suck
at the whisky flask, waiting
on the laughing owl to show
itself anew:
it grows towards morning/stillness
a fish kisses the watertop
the ripples spread to here —
all is stainless quiet
except
that stupid bird shrieking whekau! whekau!
but as soon as dawn has wrung its neck
we will regain peace and light will come
waiting on the laughing owl

Sam Hunt

My father today

They buried him today
up Schnapper Rock Road,
my father in cold clay.

A heavy south wind towed
the drape of light away.
Friends, men met on the road,

stood round in that dumb way
men stand when lost for words.
There was nothing to say.

I heard the bitchy chords
of magpies in an old-man
pine . . . *My* old man, he's worlds

away — call it Heaven —
no man so elegantly
dressed. His last afternoon,

staring out to sea,
he nods off in his chair.
He wonders what the

yelling's all about up there.
They just about explode!
And now, these magpies here

up Schnapper Rock Road . . .
They buried him in clay.
He was a heavy load,

my dead father today.

Jan Hutchison
Unwinding Matariki's Hair

Gossip about the nits in Matariki's hair
if you must, but when she kneels

close to my chair and I unwind her plaits
I see a dark forest where vines and

glossy tendrils sway a little in the breeze.
And when I sift her hair with my comb,

the comb sings the legend of a hero's love
for a woman in another sphere.

Light falls on Matariki's head
as I cup her chin with one hand
searching for nits with my other.

Gradually a clip loosens in its lock
and a key turns in our story.

Then between the snap of my thumb
and two fingers

the scissors gleam and wink around
Matariki's temples. And watch!

The wind shimmers through a filament
of hair, a filament that floats out

the window as a thread may float from
an ever-growing story.

But where is Matariki?
The moon has come from the overworld

to gaze at her.
Her head is spiked with small stars.

Kevin Ireland

Painting in the Maniototo

for Janet Frame

Since the painting looked rather too stark
for the tastes of my uncle, he had a few people
squeezed in on the curve of the road
to make it look busy, companionable.

He called for more light on the arrogant ranges
that troubled the distance, to draw
them in closer and brighten things up.
Remoteness and darkness disturbed him.

Prospects should lie within reach,
so trees became nude. Clouds were uncurtained
to open the view. Skies blushed.
The pleasing new landscape and the strangers

who came out to greet him, made the point
that a dead eye and technique weren't the be-all
and end-all of art. What was needed as well
was good taste and optimism. They enlarged you.

In my uncle's old age, he seemed oddly deflated.
His head became parched, and appeared to flatten;
more portrait than person, as though he'd been
pressed, then trimmed round the edges and framed.

A presence self-made. A shape and a shade.
A dimension forsaken. He became like the people
he bought for the road — those spectral doubles,
who were never in danger of losing their way.

Rob Jackaman

Lemons (Off Season)

for Barry Cleavin

Early July   and the suburbs of this
garden city   smell
                                        of chicken shit
a dark sprinkled libation on a thousand
herbaceous borders; round the back
vegetables   neatly
                                hulled up
                                            spars
sticking bare as wisteria out of
disadvantaged
                    beds. Old man's beard
has been gasolined to hell by the urban
ku-klux-klan
                    daubing slogans in 245T
we don't want no weeds in this here town, boy.
Domestic moggies
                        on the bonnets of cars
look distinctly   temporary
                                            that furtive
winter shuffle   that may be an attempt
to stay warm, the feline s-t-r-e-t-c-h no more
than a dim memory of previous
sensuousness. Later the frost
semi-strangulates
                        in pollution   gasping
and deep in the heart   of paradise
they've covered their lemons
                                        for the season.

You get the feeling in Riccarton
all the ships may stay buried
this year.

Anna Jackson
BADMINTON

It's not a dumb *game*, you're dumb
at it. Though it doesn't help
to say that, and you're getting
better. This is probably
the only day we'll ever get
to play like this, you realise,
it won't work in the wind, and
this is *Wellington*. We
don't have a net, we're just
counting volleys, pretty
good to hit three, then
we hit five, then our world
record of seven.
We're going for eight,
even if the clothesline
gets in the way, even if
that lunge back has me falling
backwards over the wall
that came down in the storm,
into the compost, trying to get up
in time for your next shot,
stepping further back
down the bank, stumbling
over the blackberry vine,
feeling for the concrete steps
buried somewhere under the grass,
because we've got to beat
eleven now, and although
it is getting dark, there is still
the thwack of *something*
on the strings I've hit,

and I can hear someone
stumbling down the bank
after me, hitting
something, and who
could it *be* except
for you?

Michael Jackson

The Moths

Our house had filled with moths,
a slow silting of lintel and architrave
a cupboard dust,
until I looked much closer
and found the wood-grain one,
the white quill paperbark, the blotched
shadow of a patch of bush,
an elbowing riverbank that had gone deep blue.

The soft perimeter of forests
had entered our house
fluttering around the moon.

Then for five days they drowned
in sinks and pools or seemed to wane
into sanded wood or ash on windowsills
until they became
what they were when I first noticed them:
fragments of a dull interior.

Helen Jacobs

Vessel containing

The art of painting it onto the pot —
a glaze of black sands and sunsets
mingling in brush strokes,
an estuarine flatness before the tide.

That place
that seeps across the distance to now,
seagulls circling the slipping cliffs
and falling back into the wind
that cuts —
stinging sand grains
that leave a shadow on the skin.

Black sand, grey sea, sombre orange
coloured onto the pot,
its clay shape receiving a past
not known to the potter,
my coast, long deserted and with me

where the words began.

Adrienne Jansen

Dunedin: Playing Scrabble with my aunt

She has fallen asleep
between words.
The white wave of her hair
(I always remember her
netting it in at night)
tangles the line of her letters.

Outside, yellowed birches
fidget in thin grey rain.
In here, the late dark afternoon
sits still, and waits.

She jerks up. There's a small skitter
of letters onto the board.
She builds '*handle*'
on to my '*flare*'.

My turn.
Through the window
there are purple hydrangeas
and last brown dahlias.
Rain gathers
on the washing line
in grey glass drops.

I can put '*pause*'
against her word,
or maybe '*span*'.
No, '*pause*' is better.

On the hill above,
a tall boarded house
juts its verandahs
out over the bush.
(Kinnersons', she'd said,
undertakers in town.
She remembers them all,
fathers, sons, grandsons.)
It stares down boldly
to see the next move.

It's hers.

But she's fallen asleep
again.

Louis Johnson

THE LAST CANNIBAL

You observe there are fewer characters
in what I write. A matter of taste.
Movement withers inwards. I'm seeing
fewer people. What can I draw on?
So many I've known are gone.

I have descended a long and knotted line
to the bottom of the cliff, and will never
try to scale back. Down here
the ovens are black and cold. Stones
you cannot count. No welcome

and no applause. I do not wish
to talk about it. One thing I confess.
What was once high and solitary becomes
simply lonely. I do not like the new
people. They are without qualities.

Perhaps, earlier, I was too eager
embracing precepts of the consumer age.
There is no-one left I can talk to:
none with qualities: well, it was for these
that I ate them. Memory is rich as gravy.

Mike Johnson

Up On High

1

moon hare as of old, pounding to powder his elixir of life
and the ice-bound toad
weep the sky blue

cloud palaces arise, half formed
walls aslant with a liquid, mercury gloss

jade wheels crush dew to white globules of light

moon girls shake dragon bells, girdle gems flashing
on paths heavy with cassia scent

2

dusty yellow and pristine water weave tight
beneath the immortal mountains
marking our epoch

a thousand years changing, the steady gallop
of horse-hooves

from the moon, the provinces of the Middle Kingdom
are just nine motes of dust

vast ocean depths a mere spilt cup

Andrew Johnston

The Sunflower

for Stuart Johnston, 1931–2004

One young bloom in a vase or jar, breath-
takingly yellow. And her
hands, in the morning light, the way
they arrange and rearrange. Death
brings lilies, but someone has sent a sunflower:
this is our penance, staring at the sun,
its blind eye, its ragged halo. The day,
in the end, took to its bed
before the day was over, taking thee
with it. Soon this flower, too, will be dead,
its summer of wondering done
about the sun, petal by petal: *loved me;*

didn't know how; did, unsayably so. It leaves me
as he left us, in the dark. From one breath
to the next, he'd deflect a question: in his the-
ology, *I*, *me*, *mine* were just not done.
Because he saw eye to eye with death
we can stare at the sunflower all day
but his heavenly father's garden was further
than we were prepared to go — its bed
of blood-red roses, its promises, its premises, the way
everything had been arranged; 'dead'
a manner of speaking, under the sun.
We counted ourselves lucky, hour by hour,

and by the minutes of the sunflower
(he doesn't, he does, he doesn't know me),
each in his or her own way worshipping the sun
and coming to other arrangements with death —

that it is the end, in the abstract. And then one day
someone calls, and you take a deep, deep breath.
Sister nor'wester, southerly brother —
into the mind of the man we guess our way,
blind and deaf, senseless, because he is dead.
From the end of the earth I will cry unto thee,
as daughters and sons have always done,
for words unsaid. The riverbed

was dry and I was thirsty. By your bed,
near the end, we could count our
blessings: each day,
for one thing, and though it was winter, the sun.
A sisterly sixth sense, when death
began to bloom, flew me
from the end of the earth. In a week you were dead
but we shadowed one another
through the brittle days before you went away.
You talked and talked, as you'd always done,
of all but you, till you were out of breath.
I would have liked to hear — despite your fear of the-

atre (so foolish was I, and ignorant, before thee) —
about your mother, for instance, who took to bed
when tempers rose; and how the sun
had burned a dead-
ly thirst into your father's breath;
but the hard facts I craved, my mother
knew, were the same stones, day
after day, that you buried in death-
ly silence, so that in this inscrutable way
you could build — for you, for her, for six including me —
a house, a plain, safe house, with a sunflower
in the garden. 'That which is done

is that which shall be done'
is all very well in the-
ory, but what if the sun
were black, and the book dead
wrong, and the interval under death
demanded a father
as unlike his father as day
and night? A breath
of wind reaches me
from the rose-bed;
in its vase or jar the sunflower
nods politely. Halfway

across the Channel, halfway
between waking and sleeping, my mind undone,
I had, as luck would have it, something of an inkling. The day
had been long; as I lay in the boat's narrow bed
a wave of black joy lifted me and left in me
knowledge so dark it shone. I held my breath.
Fear fell away, of death, and other
fears; the end, in the end, was the darkest jewel. I was dead
tired, and fatigue's mysterious flower
spoke perhaps in tongues. But that black sun
still shines — a talisman, obsidian, a bright antithe-
sis. Its darkness made light of death

at most, however, for me; the death
of someone else is something else. Your way
led over the border; I am a stranger with thee,
and a sojourner, but wherever I am, my place in the sun
you prepared. His earthly power
spent, your god, to us, is dead,
but it was your belief that gave us breath,
the life we take for granted every day.
What sense of your sense will I take with me?

How much of your world will we hand on?
Just before the end, on the wall beside your bed,
Peter pinned Leonardo's St. Anne. Her

smile, wry, reminds me of you, and her
hand-on-hip benevolence. Wherever death
leads, we can meet here. The power
of light in van Eyck and Vermeer. The breath
of Wallace Stevens, overhearing his way
to work. Every Henry James you read in bed,
destiny and destiny like night and day.
The valedictory music of 'The Dead'.
Thou hast set our iniquities before thee
but when all — or almost all — is said and done
sometimes it seemed you believed no less than me
that when we die we go into the sun.

There is nothing new under the sun
but much of it is mystery: this my mother knows. Her
psychological eye revised your the-
ological line. They'd converge, anyway,
at the library — your rain-cloud, your seed-bed.
You read and read and read. And saved your breath
not to write yourself, but to make each day
bloom and turn. The astonishing flower,
head full of edible seeds, bows down dead:
this is the credible sense of its death,
that here, where its turning is done
other journeys begin. It seems to me

you believed what you believed, but it strikes me,
too, that the seeds you sowed, in the mind's sun,
mattered most. (Sometimes they grew a bed
of nails: you were often 'sick to death'
of fads and feuds, the way

they shut out the sun.) Flower
of wonder, flower of might: if I see thee
on the other side, when I am dead,
I'll know there is an other
side. Till then, while we have breath,
our burgeoning work is not done:
what we have been given is a rich, difficult day

that could go on without us, nevertheless, all day,
whistling a cryptic tune. It comes to me
in the conservatory, where we catch a little sun:
I didn't know you well, and then you went away
but in the day of my trouble I will call upon thee
because you were a man to get things done.
In its vase or jar, the young sunflower
I imagine has served its purpose. Beneath its bed,
all along, the river was flowing — deep, where death
knows more than we. Sylvia dons her
gardening gloves to gather the dead
roses. Man cannot utter it, but under his breath:

'Remember me, my loves, when I am dead.'
Rest on memory's sea-bed: we will swim down to thee.
And in our own blue day, we will gaze at death
the way this one young bloom would gaze at the sun.
In the garden of the living, my mother stops for breath.
Thou thy worldly task hast done. And seeds rain from the sunflower.

Jan Kemp

Swimming

Nothing reduces you to your skin like the sea:
cold plunge into reality,
a tongue already salty
& all that power
self-propelling you through our other element,
body loving
every pummelling second,
as your mind slips on the (no wonder)
Madonna-blue beach wrap of the sky.

The straightest line imaginable
just over the breakers
visibly separating the two
doesn't exist.
You do.

Yet, can you hold
a handful of salt water
to prove it
for just one moment
before you go?

Anne Kennedy

I WAS A FEMINIST IN THE EIGHTIES

To be a feminist you need to have
a good night's sleep.

To be a feminist you need to
have your consciousness raised
and have a good night's sleep.

To be a feminist you need to
have regard for your personal well-being
have your consciousness raised
and have a good night's sleep.

To be a feminist you need to
have a crack at financial independence
have regard for your personal well-being
have your consciousness raised
and have a good night's sleep.

To be feminist you need to
champion women, have a crack at
financial independence, have regard
for your personal well-being
have your consciousness raised and
have a good night's sleep.

To be a feminist you need to do the
childminding, washing, shopping, cooking and cleaning
while your mind is on higher matters
and champion women, have a crack
at financial independence, have regard
for your personal well-being

have your consciousness raised
and have a good
night's sleep.

To be a feminist you need to button
your coat thoughtfully, do the childminding
washing, shopping, cooking and cleaning
while your mind is on higher matters
and champion women, have a crack at
financial independence, have regard for
your personal well-being, have your
consciousness raised and have
a good night's
sleep.

To be a feminist you need to
engage in mature dialogue with
your spouse on matters of domestic
equality, button your coat thoughtfully
do the childminding, washing, shopping, cooking and cleaning
while your mind is on higher matters
and champion women, have a crack at
financial independence, have regard
for your personal well-being, have
your consciousness raised and
have a good
night's
sleep.

Then a lion came prowling out of the jungle
and ate the feminist all up.

Fiona Kidman

Makara Beach, Spring

It's this skin of happiness that holds
me together. Like an olive round an anchovy's
body. More loosely, like Maggie's neck
collected in folds over her collar bone
sliding about, no special grip on the world.
A dog's life all right. But god, it's good, beside
the sea collecting wild flowers and weeds
of new zealand. Blue eyed daisies, white as foam
and dark as the sea's centre, the middle's
what counts, and yellow, there's yellow
flora all over the place. I've even got you
collecting the encroaching cream off
the land, and a smudge of silver edged
leaf. A heron
bows, arches, stalks across
stones. A bunch of overland cyclists stand
aside, smile. Indians picnic in the shade
of a cliff. A Vietnamese child lies down
waiting to be rescued on the round
rocks. A tide of gorse
flows over the hills flushed at the seams
with orange broom. We agree to share botulism
if the crayfish roll at the tearooms
should fail us. Well yes. This is certainly
short enough to be happiness.
The morning's a ball
of silk unwound about us. You gather
it back with me at its centre.

Koenraad Kuiper
from TALES

1.

When the two ambulance men
found Icarus
he was lying on a small rock outcrop
bleeding slightly.
They moved him carefully onto a stretcher,
strapped him in firmly
and brought him down to the road.
As the ambulance drove through the Cretan nightscape
Icarus gently breathed oxygen from his face mask.

The surgeon quickly noted the many fractures
the slivers of bone like icicles on the X-ray
and began the long repair.
The long bones were pinned with rods,
the joints wired,
plates placed and screwed round the larger fractures.
Under the harsh glare of the lamps
the anaesthetist tends the pale, godlike face.
Icarus breathes in unconsciousness.

He was allowed to return home,
so the legend tells,
to his people. They greeted him and said,
Sorry to hear about your accident.
He grew a black beard
and with his powerful shoulders
would push the wheelchair up to the highest point of the village,
hoist himself onto the stone wall
and stare for hours out over the storm-tossed azure sea.

2.

She turns round briefly

and strokes the cat
twice;
it is a two stroke cat;
and the broomstick lifts off.

They land in a small clearing,
set up the gear
and wait;
sure enough;

Macbeth comes by that way and hears the prophecy,
Thane of Glames, Thane of Cawdor, and shalt be King.
And he's off on his favourite horse to tell the lady
what she already knows.

In a white gown, stilly she walks the parapets.
The blood pulses darkly in her arteries.
She sees the green oak leaves brush each other.
It is late. It is late.

Leonard Lambert

A Morning Walk in the Later Days

On the muzzle of the dog
the first of grey —
so winter comes.

The silver birch —
O ever young! —
has not seen the flattened land.

My friend complains
of hungry winds
that eat away at his store of days.

His daughter, poised to fly,
is breaking news —
but the world is old.

And the garden chair I made
tells how the dead are raised —
was it six months ago, or years, or days?

Aleksandra Lane

Sold Out

for M.M.

This is the other line. Not the have you got your ticket with you
or you've pre-booked and picking it up line. This is the maybe
someone's cat will die and they won't turn up line.
The slightly unhinged
line, the crooked line. The eternally hopeful
line. The we are not in line line. We are just here
to enjoy the fresh air line. The stop staring at me line. The handicapped
boy's footy club losing and the boy telling us all about it close-up line.
This is the desperation line, the line that can easily become another, but never
disappear altogether line, one you cannot toe or heel or jump. This is also the
punch line, the democracy has gone to wait around the corner line with her ticket
crumpled in her sweaty teenage hand and her heart beating fast she gets in while
we stand outside line.

Jessica Le Bas
Two Angels

You wore the dress with the white flowers
that felt like tissue paper when you lay the seams down.

Behind he followed (business matters on higher ground).
They took your photo. He is not there in the distance.

At the wharf you climbed a wooden ladder.
He cursed because you'd gone first, wanted the lead.

The wind blew the hem of your skirt round his
nose. He held back, didn't smile. Watched his feet.

Up up up you climbed till the view of the city
was a punctuated cloud, and a sea's horizon waxed westward.

The wooden floor was littered with bird droppings.
The ceiling ached with black beams that talked of pain.

In a dark corner three bare-backed boys lay bleeding.
You said, this is as big as a boat-load of African animals.

Under the eaves of the alcove window
where a brass bell hung, he reached for your hand.

Wings grew where once there was only skin, and a cold shoulder.
You synchronised your intent to the hum of a beautiful engine.

No feathers were ruffled.

Michele Leggott
Slow Reader

the reports always said
she was conscientious but must learn
to work faster   so she outran
the reading laboratory   got through
tan to aqua and was safe at last
from the speed tests   it was a valuable
lesson   the letters dropped softly
into place making voices sing
or whisper   there was so much to
keep track of   kerning Times Roman
with a sable brush   serifs echoing
celestial geometry   hours of work
for one or two words   about time
she learned space and what lies between
compelling body and soul   light and air
song and dance   big letters flying
from keyboard to screen at a touch
marvellous sarabande   starry gavotte
freehand the camber but understand
weight and measure the way
feet walk in the world and hands
turn pages that take them
out of it again   and the copula
its even-handedness   its tying
of one thing to another so that both
spin along the causeway expanding
possibilities   a non-rival good
an open source a site for sore eyes
quick in its exchange   slow to forget
the illuminations   *psst! psssssss*
sssssss! psssssssssssssst! poem

as event   tied to the smallest detail
cut from the flying vista   alentejo
pontchartrain   beyond the river
is where we want to go   ponte littorio
shimmering into della libertà
that kind of hope   that kind of day
that one beside you
offering an arm in the dark

Graham Lindsay

River of Love

Gently, generously spoken for.
Everything streaming outwards and away —
a river from its source, the sun's radiation —
in all directions at once.

Things move round other things.
Sometimes there are collisions.

*

No matter what kind,
or the quantity of junk chucked
into it, a river has the ability to purify itself
or be purified.

A conduit streaming outwards and away,
everything streaming through us.
Each in their tiny
room a cubic
second in volume.

*

Of all the directions you could take,
this one puts you

right on the spot, first on the scene:
the victims mute round their wrecked cars
looking down through the road's
crown of shattered glass.

*

The path flows through us, love is a river,
the river of love. The landscape
bends past our brows.

Each on their tiny
sleigh of time, each in their millisecond
compartment which another

sometimes enters, sometimes enters.

Anna Livesey

Autumn Day

after Rilke

The summer has gone on
past the point of expectation.
In the afternoons now, the ngaio
shades the fish pond.
Soon the first autumn wind
will gust up from the harbour.

It is time for us to gather
the last small peaches;
for the currants to ripen against the fence,
another day or two
pressing sweetness into the fruit.

She who has left us will not come now.
If we see her at all
it will be by chance, among dry leaves,
and she will not know us.

Iain Lonie

Proposal at Allans Beach

Basalt capes
thrust into the sea, the sea
curls back intimately
into the land, celebrating
a moody marriage. The wind here
saws into flesh like cord
but just around the sandhills
a small inland sea
dotted with maimais calmly sends
the sun back to heaven.
Even in winter you can lie
on its hard white beach
naked as if you'd just crawled
up from the sea like a fish with legs
and were looking around for a mate.
But up there above the ridges
it's always going on: the air
dividing, and pouring mist
down ngaio gullies, making sheep
get up and move, unveiling contours
taking them away again.
The whole place is a test site.
I've been bringing
people here for 20 years —
sometimes with a hard question
mostly to see how we match up
to its absolute background.
It never fails. Walk with someone
from the flax-hung cliff at one end
to the tidal creek at the other
and you'll know for sure

what's biting both of you
whether you could be friends for life
and lesser domestic truths. Of course
I had to be brought here once myself
on a particularly uninviting day.
Squinting up the dark green slopes
I knew I'd come home. Later
I sat by the lagoon a whole
sunfilled September day and planned
the work of a decade. And once
I came here with a friend and the rain
blew back into our faces and told us
we could never be the lovers
we thought we wanted to be.
I'm never alone here —
the place is full of ghosts.
With luck, you might see one
swimming naked in a rock pool
on the greyest day of the year.
It is a place for strong attachments:
friends, lovers, children.
I can't promise much
but you won't forget having been here
nor who you came with, and all
that followed, if it followed.

Rachel McAlpine
Before the Fall

After the bath with ragged towels
my Dad
would dry us very carefully:
six little wriggly girls,
each with foamy pigtails,
two rainy legs,
the invisible back we couldn't reach,
a small wet heart,
and toes, ten each.

He dried us all
the way he gave the parish
Morning Prayer:
as if it was important,
as if God was fair,
as if it was really simple
if you would just be still
and bare.

Robert McLean

Springtime in America

And then, in springtime, fields of flower
began to reappear — yellow poppies
blanketed the steep upper slopes
that had been covered by chemise,
and, looking south before
the rain, there, along the fire line,
milk thistles had re-established
themselves in startling time —
once more snakes rattled, voles
and rabbit runways turned
and twisted between dense stands
of armoured spines,
where they'd refused to burn.

You said you'd seen it all before.

Still, we sat
and watched cool evening light
floating just above the ridge —
thin plumes of pink smoke drifted to the west.

And the sun began to flag
behind the hills —
thick blue smoke
from fires furthered to these eyes
scarcely touched
our sky and water.

Frankie McMillan
Developing My Father

My father has been enlarged
in a Sydenham photo shop
specializing in reproductions
and silverfish repair. He walks

with my mother down Hereford
Street. She wears a hat and tender
gloves, he wears a striped shirt,
the collar splayed like the wings

of his RSA badge. There is a war
to put behind them, shopping
to do, hungry mouths to feed.
The street photographer shoots

them wide eyed under a white sky.
For years he stores the negatives,
my mother and father
holding hands in the dark.

Cilla McQueen
Living Here

Well you have to remember this place
is just one big city with 3 million people with
a little flock of sheep each so we're all sort of
shepherds
                little human centres each within an outer
circle of sheep around us like a ring of
covered wagons   we all know we'll probably
be safe when the Indians finally come
down from the hills   (comfortable to live
in the Safest Place in the World)
                                        sheep being
very thick and made of wool and leather
being a very effective shield as ancient
soldiers would agree.
                                And you can also
sit on them of course and wear them and eat them
so after all we are lucky to have these
sheep in abundance   they might
have been hedgehogs —
                                Then we'd all be
used to hedgehogs and clothed in prickles
rather than fluff
                        and the little sheep would
come out sometimes at night under the moon
and we'd leave them saucers of milk
                                                and feel sad
seeing them squashed on the road
Well anyway here we are with all this
cushioning in the biggest city in the world
its suburbs strung out in a long line
and the civic centre at the bottom of

Cook Strait some of them Hill Suburbs
and some Flat Suburbs and some more prosperous
than others
some with a climate that embarrasses
them and a tendency to grow strange small fruit
some temperate and leafy whose hot streets lull
So here we are again in the biggest
safest city in the world all strung out
over 1500 miles one way and a little bit
the other
each in his woolly protection
so sometimes it's difficult to see out
the eyes let alone call to each other
which is the reason for the loneliness some
of us feel
and for our particular relations
with the landscape that we trample
or stroke with our toes or eat or lick
tenderly or pull apart
and love like an
old familiar lover who fits us
curve to curve and hate because it
knows us and knows our weakness
We're calling fiercely to each other
through the muffled spaces grateful for
any wrist-brush
cut of mind or touch of music,
lightning in the intimate weather of the soul.

Margaret Mahy
Bubble Trouble

Little Mabel blew a bubble and it caused a lot of trouble . . .
Such a lot of bubble trouble in a bibble-bobble way,
For it broke away from Mabel as it bobbed across the table,
Where it bobbled over Baby, and it wafted him away.

The baby didn't quibble. He began to smile and dribble,
For he liked the wibble-wobble of the bubble in the air.
But Mabel ran for cover as the bubble bobbed above her,
And she shouted out for Mother who was putting up her hair.

At the sudden cry of trouble, Mother took off at the double,
For the squealing left her reeling . . . made her terrified and tense,
Saw the bubble for a minute, with the baby bobbing in it,
As it bibbled by the letter-box and bobbed across the fence.

In her garden, Chrysta Gribble had begun to cry and cavil
At her lazy brother, Greville, reading novels in his bed.
But she bellowed, 'Gracious, Greville!' and she grovelled on the gravel,
When the baby in the bubble bibble-bobbled overhead.

In a garden folly, Tybal, and his jolly mother Sybil,
Sat and played a game of Scrabble, shouting shrilly as they scored.
But they both began to babble and to scrobble with the Scrabble
As the baby in the bubble bibble-bobbled by the board.

Then crippled Mr Copple and his wife (a crabby couple),
Set out arm in arm to hobble and to squabble down the lane.
But the baby in the bubble turned their hobble to a joggle
As they raced away like rockets . . . and they've never limped again.

Even feeble Mrs Threeble in a muddle with her needle
(Matching pink and purple patches for a pretty patchwork quilt),
When her older sister told her, tossed the quilt across her shoulder,
As she set off at a totter in her tattered tartan kilt.

At the shops a busy rabble met to gossip and to gabble,
Started gibbering and goggling as the bubble bobbled by.
Mother, hand in hand with Mabel, flew as fast as she was able,
Full of trouble lest the bubble burst or vanish in the sky.

After them came Greville Gribble in his nightshirt, with his novel
(All about a haunted hovel) held up high above his head,
Followed by his sister, Chrysta (though her boots had made a blister),
Then came Tybal, pulling Sybil, with the Scrabble for a sled.

After them the Copple couple came cavorting at the double,
Then a jogger (quite a slogger) joined the crowd who called and coughed.
Up above the puzzled people — up towards the chapel steeple —
Rose the bubble (with the baby) slowly lifting up aloft.

There was such a flum-a-diddle (Mabel huddled in the middle),
Canon Dapple left the chapel, followed by the chapel choir.
And the treble singer, Abel, threw an apple core at Mabel,
As the baby in the bubble bobbled up a little higher.

Oh, they giggled and they goggled until all their brains were boggled,
As the baby in the bubble rose above the little town.
'With the problem let us grapple,' murmured kindly Canon Dapple,
'And the problem we must grapple with is bringing Baby down.'

'Now, let Mabel stand on Abel, who could stand in turn on Tybal,
Who could stand on Greville Gribble, who could stand upon the wall,
While the people from the shop'll stand to catch them if they topple,
Then perhaps they'll reach the bubble, saving Baby from a fall.'

But Abel, though a treble, was a rascal and a rebel,
Fond of getting into trouble when he didn't have to sing.
Pushing quickly through the people, Abel clambered up the steeple
With nefarious intentions and a pebble in his sling!

Abel quietly aimed the pebble past the steeple of the chapel,
At the baby in the bubble wibble-wobbling way up there.
And the pebble *burst* the bubble! So the future seemed to fizzle
For the baby boy who grizzled as he tumbled through the air.

What a moment for a mother as her infant plunged above her!
There were groans and gasps and gargles from the horror-stricken crowd.
Sybil said, 'Upon my honour, *there's* a baby who's a goner!'
And Chrysta hissed with emphasis, 'It shouldn't be allowed!'

But Mabel, Tybal, Greville and the jogger (christened Neville)
Didn't quiver, didn't quaver, didn't drivel, shrivel, wilt.
But as one they made a swivel, and with action (firm but civil),
They divested Mrs Threeble of her pretty patchwork quilt.

Oh, what calculated catchwork! Baby bounced into the patchwork,
Where his grizzles turned to giggles and to wriggles of delight!
And the people stared dumbfounded, as he bobbled and rebounded,
Till the baby boy was grounded and his mother held him tight.

And the people there still prattle — there is lots of tittle-tattle —
For they glory in the story, young and old folk, gold and grey,
Of how wicked treble Abel tripled trouble with his pebble,
But how Mabel (and some others) saved her brother and the day.

Vana Manasiadis

Hectic Hector

Then Hector moved into the flat downstairs. He tied his Vespa

to the front gate and paid his first bond.

People said he'd been the Stay of Troy, but I couldn't see it.

He seemed restless, or preoccupied.

We could hear him pacing from the kitchen to the lounge and

back again and he fiddled with things:

his keychain, loose change, an eye pendant to ward off the bad

luck connected with fresh starts.

He kept his long hair pulled back into a ponytail, wore track

pants and old Nike sneakers.

So you see, there was really nothing very Troy-like about him

at all. Schleimann said:

his brow is not heavy enough, is not in the style of the great

warriors; and the Joneses added:

his skill with the garden shears isn't anything to write home

about. Only the Rawhitis

saw something monumental in him: What ponytail eh?

Hector's hair's in a tikitiki-top-knot

bang on his crown; has a peacock feather sticking out of it

and a bone comb.

Whatever the truth of it,

he got into the habit of collecting old radio parts. He filled the flat

with wires, transistors,

amassed large quantities of knobs and dials. Mum worried:

who is going to clean up

this *chaos* when Hector go? This *confusion*, as it looks to me?

But she needn't have.

Hector tidied every last inch on the night before he moved out.

He put the finishing touches

on his ham radio, vacuumed up all unnecessary fragments,

checked his pendant and left the key in the lock.

Over the years, if we turned the dial of our radio too far left by mistake, we'd find Hector

talking to elderly relatives, listening to news of wars and soccer

wins, betrothals and wakes.

In short, staying in touch over the short waves.

He never went

back for a visit; he bought a three bedroom house (with sea

views) in Maupuia,

and a Honda Chariot, in which he'd sometimes go for drives

around the bays.

Bill Manhire

Kevin

I don't know where the dead go, Kevin.
The one far place I know
is inside the heavy radio. If I listen late at night,
there's that dark, celestial glow,
heaviness of the cave, the hive.

Music. Someone warms his hands at the fire,
breaking off the arms of chairs,
breaking the brute bodies of beds, burning his comfort
surely to keep alive. Soon he can hardly see,
and so, quietly, he listens: then someone lifts him
and it's some terrible breakfast show.

There are mothers and fathers, Kevin, whom we barely know.
They lift us. Eventually we all shall go
into the dark furniture of the radio.

Selina Tusitala Marsh

Two Nudes on a Tahitian Beach, *1894*

Gauguin,
you piss me
off.

You strip me bare
assed, turn me on my side
shove a fan in my hand
smearing fingers on thigh
pout my lips below an
almond eye and silhouette me
in smouldering ochre.

I move
just a little
in this putrid breeze
hair heavy to
fuscous knees, still
I'm the pulse
on the arm of this wall
and I've drawn her to me again.

Here she comes.

Not liking that she likes me
not liking you, but knowing that she
likes me, not liking you
liking me, but she
likes me and sees me,
but not you,
because you
Gauguin,
piss us
off.

Courtney Sina Meredith

HOMELAND

You get back everybody says *oh you're back!*
You are back but everything has moved.
You are an old woman you are a concrete crow
you are a set of lilac limbs.

Everybody says *tell me about somewhere?*
You are the plentiful remains of war fought towns.
You get to sleep one night and then the next.
Everybody thinks you dream in foreign prose.

Everybody knows you are back.
Everybody sees your body in the city in the arms of friends.
You are a silver canal you are a young rose
you are a path grown men skate.

Everybody stands in front of you like a mirror.
They do their hair in your face *so good you're back!*
You are certain in the seeing of what appears whole.
You are a nought you are a track you are a bone.

You are waiting to come home.
You are waiting to come home.
You are waiting to come home.

Karlo Mila

Eating Dark Chocolate and Watching Paul Holmes' Apology

i am sucking on a sante bar / sneaked / bought at pak'n'save
in a cigarette gold wrapper / i remember when you bought
them in dairies / they were stripped and served undressed /
edges worn from the friction / getting down with the
brown / chocolate dust was in the air

i am watching paul holmes apologise for calling kofi annan a
darkie / darkie takes me back to

6 years old / school grounds / see-saws / we won the
war / we won the war in 1944 / mean boys alternating
between catch and kissing and sticks and stones / darkie /
tania got called blackie / golliwog / i remember being
thankful i was pretty and fair / and had long hair / no one
called me manu off playschool or darkie / i was a milk
chocolate glass and a half / half caste / caramello enough to
be safe from bitter dark accusations

tonight paul holmes apologised for calling kofi annan a
darkie / takes me back to

10 years old / sitting on my dad's stomach / him flat on the
sofa / we're watching a week night movie / southern
drawls and white sheets / me crying hot wet tears over
black men with hurt in their eyes / what does lynching
mean maka? / my daddy / dark / my feet dangling off his
tummy / me milky brown chocolatey sweet / wanting
to grow up and be the prime minister / or a lawyer like
matlock / make everything all right for darkies everywhere

tonight paul holmes apologised for calling kofi annan a
darkie / takes me back

15 years old / barry / surf lifesaver / washboard abs /
the mattel man / automatic winking machine / ambivalent
crush / half hate / half fetish / blonde frosting in his fringe /
darkies / that's what he called us / hope you don't mind
darkies / he said / setting up his mate / flirting on the phone

tonight paul holmes apologised for calling kofi annan a
darkie / takes me back

17 years old / do you think they would ever let a boonga
be prime minister / corey p / dreadlocked bob marley
wannabe / says to me / mocking laughter / he's drunk at
three / in highbury / but we never dreamed they'd let an
indian woman be mayor of dunedin / so let's sukhi it to
them corey p / we were darkies anonymous then / making
fun of ourselves before anyone else could / revolution in
the bottom of a bong / cutting off our veins to spite our
lives /

tonight paul holmes apologised to the nation

i am 28 / aucklander / jokes about jaffas don't involve
maoris and minis / just another f-ing aucklander / the
p.i.'s here outnumber prejudice in wide open spaces /
skinheads low key / less closely shorn / too much rugby
league brawn / on the arms of coconuts / i've been told
i'm the cream rising to the top / the cream of the crop /
nesian queen / rank and file member of the chocolate
soldier movement / getting down with the brown /

tonight paul holmes apologised

sorry / he said / i've hurt my family / i may have hurt
yours /

yes / we scrapped in the car over it / there was yelling / by
the time we got to the end of the mangere motorway / i
was crying / who is this redneck with the big brown
shoulders sitting next to me / anti pc / darker than me /
defending freedom of speech / but i don't want it to be all
right /

/ i don't want my kids to have stanzas of darkie memories /

sorry / paul holmes said / i could see that he meant it / i felt
sad for him / and happy / i signed the petition to say he
should get sacked / i am a manager in a govt department /
not matlock / not the pm / just a member of the chocolate
soldier movement / melting in the middle

David Mitchell

A Letter

I am here my love
beneath an apricot sky.

Summer is a young girl,
her voice is thick

in these green islands.

The valley gorse was burning
last week. Quietly in the night.

Tonight it is warm. Just a song bird
and the hills.

It is not lonely, but very slow.

I am here my love.
This is all

my beauty.

Harvey Molloy

Battle of San Romano

Vasari once saw
a destroyed cartoon
for the centre panel
of Uccello's *Battle of San Romano*
which depicts in the background
a young scholar
distracted from reading
by the clamour of the battle.

Faint pencil strokes
outline
a hesitant gaze
as he chooses between
the pleasures of his book
or recording the scene.

Later sketches
show him on the summit
of a distant hill
sitting back
against a matchstick tree
trousers unbuttoned
seduced by the written
he reads
while on the fields below
plasticine horses
snort at their opponents.

The battle
we are told
was a bloody one

the fate of the scholar
unknown.

Elizabeth Nannestad

Facing the Empty Page

The empty page
looks all innocence
but has its own sense of humour.

You might decide
to call yourself Mme X, be sighted in foreign cities without forwarding address.
The empty page will be at home, waiting.

The empty page is
the Inquisition: you could throw yourself upon it,
say, *save me.*

The empty page has
no heart
no home
no pity.

The empty page takes
everything you can give it, still is only satisfied, if ever
for a very short time.

It is a mistake to introduce the empty page
to your prospective lover. It will spoil everything
leaving you alone, just you and the empty page, forever.

Don't be a fool for it,
the empty page.
Take refuge in supermarkets

with two radios and a loudspeaker
playing at once.
The empty page can't stand children's cartoons on television

so turn up the volume.
Give the controls to a person aged less than three
who'll be a match for it,

the empty page. Yet
neither will it be
set aside indefinitely.

The empty page is closely related to the Great Australian Desert.
Good men, good women, died trying to cross it.
Some people find that encouraging.

The empty page
haunts the O.K. Corral
looking for someone, might as well be you, to gun down.

The empty page is
some people's idea of desirable
and not unwilling

to come round for a short time to your way of thinking.
The empty page will
settle in

take your name at the bank
drink your whisky
inhabit your house

while you'll feed on your own fingernails
wear black
suffer doubt.

The empty page will retain affection, so long as you don't
shove it, whack it, thrash it, push it around
or make crossings out.

The empty page, it's hell
to live with.
And to live without.

Emma Neale

Well

Afterwards, I stood with my child
on the river's bridge
over the storm-swollen rapids.

Make your two wishes, he said,
and into my hands he pressed
shredded petals he'd found, fallen
from the peach-silk hot house flowers
he calls 'the singing plant'
for their glorious, open mouths.

Their colour flared like tossed coins
towards the river's turbulent surface:
on contact still they burnt a moment
like soft metal lit by air —
then were pulled beneath the bridge and gone.

What did you wish? he asked, as we walked on —
and I could have confessed each one:
your name, and what I wanted, still want
to have you choose to say: but then as good admit

I wished to be like water:
able to take whatever fractures it —
floodwrack, oar-thrust, fish leap,
the birds' swift javelin stabs
as they hurtle down and pierce its skin —
and to then as smoothly mend again,
unmarred,
as if the mind could be its own physician.

John Newton

Opening the book

You open the book
and there unfolds a road   its skin is blue, it is summer
the heat   that dances in its hollows turns

into water. You ride it in the vehicles of strangers:
homesteads and haybarns   dusty yellow sheeptrucks
convoy of soldiers in jungle greens returning

from an exercise
slipping past their polarised windscreens;
you draw from them splinters   of lives made of words

though you never take your eyes off the mountains.
The mountains   reach out to embrace you
they fold their blue ankles

they give birth to rivers, they
can even crouch like tigers if that's the way you
want them: they are a story you tell

about yourself, a story you are journeying
into, that swallows you.   You leave
the road, then   you honour the logic of ridges

and gorges, of funnels, of slotted
stone chimneys   You startle a huge bird
nesting in the riverbed, climbing on slow

cream and ash coloured wings   and you follow
as it disappears
inland, you tunnel to the spine of the island

and bury yourself   alive, with your possessions, this
curved sky, this whisper of ice-cloud
this magic mountain shutting behind you.

James Norcliffe

The Gentle Art of Manipulation

we talked of the turtle eggs in the market
sagging in baskets like soft ping pong balls

the beaches of glassy sand white and shining
the streaming jellyfish rampant in the clear water

like those other examples of referred pain
the aching ulna from the fused cervical vertebrae

the woman standing lost in the driveway
eyes shaded and oblivious to the traffic noise

and the question must again be asked:
what price can be put on the healing touch

on fingers that can feel the source of things
the reassuring pressure that can persuade

a film to run slowly backwards for a gentle time
or rain to rise steadily to billowing clouds

Gregory O'Brien

House and Children

Our friends have ways
of describing
their children, their names

a house for them to move
into, or a door for you
to knock upon: Gretel

'like metal' or Galatea
'parts of your body
you touch to make you laugh'.

Imogen, a name, like 'imagine'
I have walked around
and around that name too.

But can you ever
circumnavigate
a word? Or even a letter? A 'g'

like a wave of the sea, its one twisted leg
gone all the way
around? Naming children, you say,

is like buying a house. You shouldn't
believe what
they tell you you tell yourself,

those people for whom 'good light'
means a hole in the roof.
And you'll have to stand your friends

on a chair on the back lawn
for the sliver
of blue those people call

an ‘expansive sea view’. But
is the sea ever less
than expansive? Remember

you’re buying a house
not a zen monastery.
A house not a scaffolding

to hang wallpaper from.
A house, the walls to stop those you love
falling out of your life.

John O'Connor

A Left Hook

an early experience
of the left hook (admirably

tight if open handed) came
at the beatific hand of

Monseigneur O'Dea — too
old to be a parish priest — who

about to impart the very
body & blood of Christ found I

was not holding the paten
correctly, a few years later

an equally irascible boxing
coach imparted impeccable

advice on how to throw it,
though he didn't know the bit

about feinting with Jesus.
when the good monseigneur

had his final photo taken
he bestowed a copy on our family

— old friends should be so blessed —
for a decade it sat on the mantelpiece

between a bunch of plastic grapes
& a glass bowl that snowed if shaken.

Maris O'Rourke

On Being Told I'm To Be a Grandmother: a Villanelle

So — do I have to be responsible again,
revisit parenting and refind the way
to enjoy the journey and embrace the pain?

Will it mean a great need to constrain
my tramping, reading, writing every day,
do I *have* to be responsible again?

Can I watch their every move and bear the strain
of daily love and care, come what may?
Can I enjoy this journey and embrace the pain?

Well maybe I can be an *Auntie Mame*,
we'll climb mountains in Nepal and USA
and I'll learn to be responsible again.

Plus I remember how love can wax and wane,
and you don't care what you have to pay,
you do enjoy the journey and embrace the pain.

I dream him in my arms and know I'll gain
from lifting, cuddling, playing. In my own way
I can be responsible again.
I *will* enjoy the journey and embrace the pain.

Peter Olds

Under the Dundas Street Bridge

People when they ask us, Where do you live?
We tell them, Under the Dundas Street bridge.

They laugh. They cannot see what we can see:
bottles, eels, mattresses, paradise ducks floating

downstream. They can't see how cosy we can be
with just a fire, our faggots of sticks, our sandwiches,

our coffee cups and books. They don't know we
have candles and blankets and problems with the

doormat like everyone else. They can't see
the other side with its weeds and stormwater pipes

thick with stormwater . . . People when they ask us, What
do you eat? We tell them, Eels, bottles, puha and mattresses.

They don't see the flow of visitors, the koha of bread,
baked beans and eggs. They weren't there the night

the river flooded and took away our nasturtium plants. They
wouldn't know the time it took us to put the house back

in order; the bickering over the last cigarette, the hospital
visits, the power failure, the shock when the doctors closed

our case — and we, stranded on opposite sides of the river
not talking: the river stripping everything we had between us

leaving us hugging our knees like two canvas bags tied with
string . . . People when they ask us, Why are you happy?

We tell them, Bottles, eels, mattresses; Vicks VapoRub,
long hair and comics. When the phone rings we let it

ring; when the gas-man calls we let him in; we share
our cigarettes with strangers; we eat porridge every day;

the gas-man is our friend, he gives us gas on credit —
we wouldn't be without it . . .

People when they ask us, Why do you live
under the Dundas Street bridge? We tell them . . .

Bob Orr

CALYPSO

On such a night as this
when the moon is a long boat
dancing between pohutukawa branches
shall we go sailing in it?
Outside our window the tide must now be rising.
It's ours for the asking.
Some stars we'll take for sugar
some we'll take for salt
that way everything should be to our taste.
We could be gone by the morning
to some calypso coast —
an island offshore
where even the waves are dancing
and where the fish most surely will be leaping.
Just say the word
and I'll tell you I'm not dreaming.

Chris Orsman

A Colonial Farewell

Port Chalmers, New Zealand
Tuesday 29 November 1910

History's a flammable nitrate
the cameraman gathers in

with a sweeping roll-call
— a sixty-second pan

across the decks, the docks,
the crowd's mouthing cheer.

What burns in him
a loving prescience

is the great good humour
of the crew. Here they come

joking, filling pipes
— self-created men

transcendent in their moods
who lean a little towards poetry.

On this blithe day no one will guess
who will be famous among them,

who will survive and be forgotten:
soldiers, sailors, scientists,

subscribers to the funds.
At noon they cast off from the wharf;

beyond the framework of the shrouds
the twentieth century slips by.

The *Terra Nova* turns upon its axis
— the fixed eye of the kinematograph —

masts and funnel align
as she steers to the harbour mouth.

The Captain paces the fo'c's'le,
his blue eyes crease as he grins

against a backdrop of southern hills,
the strikedown of rigging.

The print ghosts and jerks,
the cameraman cranks away.

Vincent O'Sullivan

Seeing You Asked

There's a dozen things I might tell you.
There is a Chinese poem to begin with
of a woman folding curtains as she leaves
a man, forever. There is a Roman writing
from the edge of ice-fields, a vista
of dull silver beyond clicking reeds,
to a woman who watches a blue smoking
mountain in almost unbearable heat.
There are wartime movies with sad bridges
across morning rivers, the woman pressing
the two wings of her collar together
as a train draws out. There's the story
as well of a woman driving north
towards a lake, a lake that was once fire,
a house by the lake, a life inside the house,
where today's love becomes another fiction
you open when the room is empty,
put down when you hear voices, stand
up, smiling, at life where it happens . . .
There is no ending to certain stories,
the plot has no desperate turns, the vase
on the bedside table burns with azaleas
whatever happens. But love, we say,
love, there are corners on the stairways,
there are fragments in each hour,
when the notes drift back, the ones
scarcely heard — just as the lake is always
beside you, spreading out, and out.

You say you swim, you read, you fish.
There is something like the glint of a hook,
there is something, love, in that shimmering
vault, trolling too fast to speak of.

Alistair Paterson

Laying Your Ghost

I'm trying to lay your ghost — the poltergeist
that every morning rattles on my roof, shakes
windows, doors — the blinds — and throws into my head
a miscellany of things I'm not supposed to remember,
that common-sense insists should have been forgotten
by the end of November or — if not quite that early —
at least in January when the New Year's almost done
and less persistent poltergeists vanish into the sun.

The fault, of course, is mine — not yours: your
doppelganger I've invented for myself — raised by
speculation, incantation, wishful-thinking, put through
its gymnast motions by a secret act of will —
but now the spectre's self-directing and you move
about the house entirely of your own volition,
demonstrating with table rapping and an occasional
broken glass, your obvious and unexpected power.

Four hundred miles away — a little more or less —
and plainly innocent, you do the things you do:
go shopping on the Quay, climb up Plimmer's Steps,
entertain a visitor, reconsider, change your mind,
and sometimes — if the occasion's suitable — pursue
the self-same speculation I'm indulging in myself,
ask why it is that everything inevitably turns out
to be exactly as it is and never something else.

I could use hypnosis, might possibly pretend
that nothing ever happened or, if that doesn't work,
persuade myself such happenings don't really count:
in fact, I'm trying to lay your ghost — have studied

all the books and drawn a careful pentagon, lit
the ritual candles, sealed the windows and the roof —
your poltergeist is laughing, your *doppelganger* knows
you've got the kind of spectre exorcism can't remove.

Kiri Piahana-Wong
THIS IS IT

One day you're just
sitting there, doing something
that's not particularly
important, and the clouds
glacing the sky capture
your attention, and you
realise, with a start, that
this is it, this is
the shape of your life.

All these years waiting to
grow into something
fabulous, fitting, but
instead, just growing
bigger.

Not knowing what it
is that you want
anymore, or what
it isn't.

Too many things defined
by absences — the phone
that doesn't ring, the
empty fruit bowl. All
so mundane, not like
the absent lover you have
always dreamt of
having. Being possessed
by.

And now the starlight
pours down on your
face, millions of
light-years too late.
They're already dead.
But look. Look
how brightly they
shine.

Sugu Pillay

ST HELIERS

One toe dipping into the black paint
she steps into the canvas
no consoling light
from café windows opposite
where once they held hands
& supped the sea's virtual puns
then a brilliant picture
now a flattened perspective
lovers affirm reality by their flight
into one dimensional borders on Grecian urns
frozen but sustained by *Being-in-Time*

And now the dreamy landscape leaps away
the red runs right through the blue
casting mauve shadows on stars
falling into the drowning sea
as the waves die on her *palette of blobs*

& Time always sets with Robbie Burns
whose June rose spreads its scarlet
in shock waves spinning out
from the darkening Rangitoto

Its once radiant node
the composing eye of this seascape
dims like wounded Bhishma
on his bed of arrows

Swinging in & out of her eyeline
the sails have sunk her gaze
stranded like a pilot whale
on Farewell Spit

Who rides so late in the night
and wind?

Galaxies of women . . .

Virginia's mermaid continues to sit
on her rock *with a pad on her knee*
saving a page for the relentless sea
surging in

Her shadow stretches
from Mission Bay to St Heliers

The problem of space has not found
its proper articulation
or that of time's *textes pour rein*
since all movement is towards loss

Beckett artfully transferred stones
from pocket to pocket to the mournful tune
we cannot know & we cannot be known
Virginia would have told him
stones drown in women's pockets

Mark Pirie

THREE SHORT FILMS (WITH '*LANDSCAPE*' INCLUDED)

1 'NATIONALISM'

for some time
the males lurk out there
on their new land,
discovering their 'authenticity'

they have taken
their compasses, their maps,
and their egos:

everything's Kiwi
everything's British
everything's Pakeha
everything's 'hard'

while to the left of set,
a young man with cue cards
continues to remind us

it will be a 'perilous journey'
for all those who undertake
to speak in their language

or, at the very least,
follow in their footsteps.

2 'THE DRESS CODE'

below the rough clefts
and folds of the valley,

a painter's easel
awaits its princess
and unicorn.

within the frame:
a macrocarpa and some gorse
in need of a good trim.

yet when the figures
finally gallop into view,
we are surprised to find
a New York gangster

somewhat obscured
by a billboard
reading 'Coke'
against the sky.

the man, appearing
at the 'right time'
in the 'wrong place',
seems voluntarily nonchalant,

and, as he scratches his head
to decline our language,

we can't help but focus on
the shining steel
gripped (to perfection)
in his hand.

3 'A MAINLAND POW-WOW ON THE SWAG'

there are hills,
a drizzle of bush,
some native trees,
and an evening sun.

we follow three figures
as they fix their billy
beside the camp-fire.

one cracks open a Speights,
the other jokes, and the third
clasps his Swanndri neatly.

(he might not even be there.)

we respond with a click
'for our friends back home'
and then flash our backstage passes

when we finally meet
there'll be 'handshakes all round'.
and the jugs'll be on the house.

Vivienne Plumb
Vic's Dick

Spring in the stacks
and the librarians leap like lambs,
I can smell oranges
deep in the shelves while I search for
Steinberg's *Sexuality of Christ*
in Renaissance Art, every loincloth is tumescent
and Lazarus raised himself in more ways than one.

Spring, and the students know, they understand,
they are hidden in the stacks sucking
their oranges, that year round jasmine
of the library; their inky digits
dig and scrape at the fragrant pockled peel,
those cannibals eat the flesh and leave the rinds
in artistic installations from 746 to 800.09.

Outside in the spring wind
a Japanese man struggles with the door
of his sunny yellow mitsubishi,
lovers embrace, and inside in the stacks
the students are one masticating army
with their doorstop sandwiches, drawing
pricks and balls in the art books,
wanking in the basement,
they insert crude words
cum cunt bonk on the database
stupid dick: the messages
rise as reborn phoenix
if you hit buttons sixty nine
not sixty six. The stacks smell
of broken shoes, condoms, and gum wrappers,

articles of used clothing,
and empty gatorade bottles.

A tweedy professor stumbles
over the white diagonals of Kelburn Parade,
his hair is eccentric tufts,
they're koalas, frill-necked lizards,
side stepping side swiping takahe,
but behind them the scribbling and swearing
and innuendo continues, foul Middle English mouths
that steal the soap, and graffiti in the loos.

The graffiti is curlicued, poetic, bellicose,
coprologic, occasionally succinct, sometimes religious,
felt tipped over the back of the loo doors
and walls it is the scatology of the universe,
the emptying of the bladder encourages philosophy.
The students have claimed their own indemnities
tattooed for the future into the wood:
Tutor destruct button or *they shoot lecturers don't they*
and on that back desk in MacLaurin
Vic has no dick.

Lindsay Pope

OUTPOST

MARCH, 1941.

The coast is a scribble. Stars are stored in a wooden box on my shelf. It is more black than white here. Like algebra but colder.

The hut's walls are a ghetto of mice. Those I catch become whiskers of smoke in the firebox.

I attend to the scratching radio.

This is not my dream.

JULY, 1942.

The short days are long here. Morse code stutters in my aerial.

Every door of the home of the wind has been thrown open. An albatross turns the world on a dip of its wing. It has learnt the axioms of the air.

Mice crawl in the pockets of my sleep.

I wake, clutching a stick of chalk. Each day a tally mark.

DECEMBER, 1943.

The mice have all but disappeared.

Clouds, black as slate, are heavy with names. They fall upon roof clutching ash.

On short wave the radio coughs all night long.

I have lost the frequency.

Jenny Powell

Love in the Early Winter

I open the window
and breathe in so much air
that the rest of the world pauses
through lack of oxygen.
I am gulping in the serenity
of early winter in the morning.
There's no bustle of breeze
so the grasses are still,
and the water race is duty bound
to reflect a frame of land.
This is the best season for light,
which flings itself
in acrobat angles on whatever
takes its fancy.

The view spreads
up the valley and waits
by the hills.

Joanna Preston

Parable of the Drought

He got up from the narrow bed
and shaved off his beard,
rinsing his face and the razor
with a last mugful of fresh water.
He dressed, and waited
for sunlight through the window
to wake the boy.

They walked all morning,
following the sun and the line
of fenceposts that shimmered west.
He looked only once at the sky,
shading his eyes
when a black cockatoo flew overhead.

When they came to broken country
the bloodwood and gidgee
sucked the shade back into themselves.
Heat smashed against the gibbers.

He kissed the boy's forehead
and held his skinny shoulders,
breathing his scent of smoke and dust and sweat
and a sweetness
that for a moment could have been his wife.
He slid his fingers into the boy's hair
— *just like a wether*, he thought, *just like a ewe* —

He watched until the boy's eyes
lost their brilliance — the same brittle blue
as the sky that even now
refuses to cloud.

Chris Price

Keeping Ravens

After the flood, the boat's white
breastbone rests, exhausted
on dazzling water. We have

survived, as we knew
we would, to work our way
through freeze-dried food

and scan the unpredictable
tide. Below, the latest
calculating instruments purr

in their cool hutches.
Yet despite satellites
and our confidence

in the boat's design
at the last we could not
leave behind our old companions.

The ravens were carried on
in swaying cages, their
coarse monosyllables drifting

back to those on shore.
Now on deck our winged
dark contradictions hang

as navigation lights against
the sea's relentless glare.
Our devices offer

no new information.
Disconsolate, we slump
against the hatch and listen

to the low and constant gossip
of our gallows-wives.
We must resolve

to let the ravens go.
From Noah we know
they're not to be relied on,

may settle for bloated islands, corpses
on which to perch
and feed, and never return.

But from Floki we know
they just might find
some hard bright

sliver of hope, that we
may finally stumble down
a crude gangplank

to curse and steady
uncertain sea legs
on ice-encrusted land.

John Pule
from The Hurricane Love Songs

14

I woke up to find a butterfly across your mouth
you were dressed in those oriental jackets
which tricked me into believing dragons sufficed
so I scrawled a poem onto the wall

how I reached these shores on the *Maui Pomare*
some white girl, impressed with what I wrote
tore the wallpaper off and ran, I watched
as she ran with maps and charts to my destination

I called out, only half of me belongs here,
she stops, looks back, deep in thought, what do you mean,
she replies, thinking twice about the wallpaper

the land, as I walk towards her, and how
it does not decide who should die or be buried,
before I reach her, only words remained of her flight

Sarah Quigley

To Waitemata Harbour

You have such
clever hands.

You hold the islands
on the tips of your
fingers, lightly so

you never submerge
them. Firmly enough that
they don't float away.

If a person could hold
another person like that —
well, then

there would only be
love.

Maggie Rainey-Smith

At Katherine's Bay

Water washes over the road
at Eastbourne while

latte spume licks the heels of
city jeeps. The southerly lifts sand

and little blue penguins invade
the investment, once were holiday homes

where Katherine stayed and Stanley Burnell's
children played their part,

native bush and real estate collide
in Sunday kaleidoscope sunshine.

Jonathan Trout isn't shouting out
from the waves nowadays

he sits instead, in the shelter of the boatshed
and watches Stanley catch the ferry.

Linda feasts on eggs florentine
and Beryl's no longer afraid

the Kembers' brittle laughter
can be heard over barbecues

and in the bush, if you listen carefully
from somewhere in the shadows

you can hear Jonathan saying,
It's all wrong, it's all wrong.

Richard Reeve

Summer Wedding

for Adrian

Winding among reeds, wind that once had blown
Through land on which an age of shadows passed,
Confronts the hub of something hard and new.
The barest protest of some tread-turned stone —
A crunch of rubber rounding down the schist
From which the crest of mountain ranges grew —
Is swamped beneath the sold seas of the dew.

Nothing shows up, no march, no lords of rain
Will break the lines of cars that swarm the hill;
The middle class has come to claim its view.
Eight-bedroom houses stare across the plain.
The brokers join the hawk to make their kill.
Children observe their parents waltzing through
The lounge-room suite towards the barbecue.

For most, such pleasures are the point of life.
No higher purpose tracks the rouge-smudged ape
That wanders through the garden with a glass
Half-primed to make its owner someone's wife.
The mountains leave their interesting shape
On darkling fields, for white men in the grass
(To bare their souls before they make a pass).

I dream the slow demise that marks my kind.
The morning burns like conscience on the house
Where couples swelter, writhing in each bed,
Though sunlight scarcely penetrates the blind.
They come; they go. The everlasting spouse
Confers his blessings on each shrouded head.
The breeze reserves its laughter for the dead.

Nicholas Reid
Bluff Seas

Skewed on a tip of rock
the straps of copper-coloured kelp
dance in the noon sea's swell.

A slowly-shaken piupiu swings
out and in, on the rock's hip,
by the tide's easy forceful breathing.

Nature's rough edge is softened
in the warm, wet soup of copper
colour over steel-blue depth.

Disjecta membra, they were wrenched
from their dark submarine forest
and drifted up to die.

Their dance is a death dance.
Soon they will putrefy and stink,
and hikers think dead weed is ozone.

Warm mammal blood in a cold sea,
a pod of dolphins butt through
hordes of surface-resting seabirds.

The horizon's mutton-birding islands
are aircraft-carriers;
the line of sky unarguable.

Helen Rickerby
from Abstract Internal Furniture

Theodora
takes her voice out
of her throat, gently
puts it in a small wooden
box painted with stars and
moons, and closes the
catch
firmly.

she takes her spare
smile out of a
drawer, where it has been
nestling amongst silk
scarves. it is
made of ceramic and
is painted a glossy
red. she attaches it
to her mouth with
a little
glue.

Theodora is creating herself

theodora is being created

Theodora puts on a dress
made of gossamer web
and peacock eyes.
venus hangs
from one ear and
pluto from
the other.

Harry Ricketts

The Necessity of Failure

Why this obsession with success,
which brings so brief a glow?
Fading already: won; done it;

gone. Afterwards, what then? What next?
With failure, there's so much
more to savour, so much more to feel.

Like a loose tooth, you can jiggle
it any time you like;
the true friend you can never brush off.

Failure is like having children:
you find out stuff about yourself
you'd never known nor dared to guess.

And think of the variety.
There are so many ways
to fail. Not just the smart disasters

like going bust or off your head,
betraying those you love
or knowingly blowing your talent —

only a few of us can be
that chic. Don't be choosey.
Any flop will reward you with guilt,

remorse, embarrassment and shame,
whose every nuance
you can endlessly replay, retaste.

Even quite a tiny failure
can last you a lifetime:
that thing you said, that moment you missed,

will twist in time until you see
how it led to all that
and all of this. Some revelation.

So don't begrudge your blunders,
screw-ups, A minor blues.
Nothing's wasted; failure makes sense.

Jack Ross

Trying to Write

Trying to write a poem called 'Things
to Do in Auckland When You're
Dead' while watching *Barton*
Fink I find the pencil
necks are ganging
up on me
again
de-
vising
scripts for a-
ments to deform
unlike the other writers
hard at work on Wallace Beery
wrestling flicks . . . Let's put a stop to that
right now

Bill Sewell

By Ships We Live

It was a tingling in the balls that told them,
like edging too close to a rock face:

a twist of the tide, the slop of the swell,
the mercenary attentions of seabirds.

Out of the blue they broke,
the sails, the expectations, the names.

Takitimu, *Heemskerck*, *Endeavour*:
how they transported their history

as a deadening freight, as baggage,
barnacles clinging like grievances to the keel.

Then the commerce would begin:
footprints for sand; words for silence.

There, not just as the unusual event,
the sudden flaw on the curve,

but by the month, by the day,
feeling their way along the chart

for that orifice in the cliffs
and making their run through the heads:

Orpheus, *Tararua*, *Penguin*,
all finding out just how intolerant

of carelessness this coast can be,
once you sail out of line.

Yet the masts still thickened ashore,
the funnels exhaled bad faith

(according to the terms of the bargain).
While men went below as into a mine

to dig out the lampblack
that darkened their days and their lungs

and the names of the ships that carried it:
Korowai, *Myrtlebank*, *Asunçion de Larrinaga*.

Iain Sharp

The Ponsonby Strut

First you go downtown and you get half-cut.
You climb College Hill when the taverns shut,
find an open party and talk some smut
or politics or art or God knows what.
Smoke in your eyes and cheap wine in your gut —
that's how you do the Ponsonby Strut,
whoa-ho-ho the Ponsonby Strut (yeah).

Now here's the hoop-la — the cast's all present:
the drunks the punks, the poets, the peasants,
the incoherent, the incandescent,
the refugees from Boyle Crescent,
the drugged, the bugged, the insipid, the incessant,
the fresh-from-rehab semi-convalescent,
the unhappily unhugged, the plain unpleasant,
and Herman (the world's oldest adolescent),
who boasts to his hosts he's still tumescent.
There's an implant down his urethra, but
it doesn't impede the Ponsonby Strut,
whoa-ho-ho the Ponsonby Strut.

On the porch by the flowering quince
in fake black leather the Dark Prince
trills of his talent, tries to convince
Rhiannon with the raspberry rinse
that he's the tastiest morsel since
lasagne added cheese to mince.
Rhi just yawns; the rest of us wince
beneath the moon's wan aquatints.

Distant galaxies lure us, but
we keep on doing the Ponsonby Strut,
whoa-ho-ho the Ponsonby Strut.

In the hall beneath the gilt chandelier
Hollywood Lorna strives to make it quite clear
she inhabits the wrong hemisphere.
She's a born star, she says. Did you see her last year
in the outdoor production of King Lear?
But even while Lorna is bending your ear
Con, the red-nosed Trotskyite pamphleteer,
clutching fresh pamphlets attacks from the rear.
You look for a nook in which to disappear.
You just popped in, after all, for the beer
and whatever else you could souvenir.
The cost some evenings is too great, but
short of emigrating to Lower Hutt,
what else can you do but the Ponsonby Strut?
whoa-ho-ho the Ponsonby Strut.

Well, first you get sloshed as a halibut,
then swim up College Hill with your eyes half-shut.
Cursing yourself for being such a slut,
you crash another party and say God knows what.
Martian canals in your eyeballs,
cardboard wine in your gut;
that's how you do the Ponsonby Strut.

Kerrin P. Sharpe

Mining the Heart

the cardiologist
wears his own heart
like antlers

today he pushes
a metal trolley
through yards of arteries
to weed your heart

wings of old newspapers
canary claws
a scapular feather
cover the sign
you are entering the heart

a workplace where there
is always the anvil
the heat of hammers

the beetle mallet
its repetition a lantern
of pulley and flywheel
joins the fury of blood

as carts of forgotten sunlight
fall on your wrist
the cardiologist
removes his davy lamp
and closes the valve

Elizabeth Smither

Leaf Flurry Tram

On Dandenong Road the white tram
throws up the autumn leaves
to not-quite window height.

Those inside are unaware
of what beauty follows them —
leaves from the track dancing up

in the passing current of air
and staying suspended
until the eddy moves on

and fresh (dried) leaves take their turn
to levitate for this great wizard
the East Brighton tram

on its way to University
white as a bride
with a veil billowing

in the speed of passage
the tracks that lead to
a bliss not in front of us

but behind, a double
blessing, made more beautiful
because we don't see it.

C. K. Stead

Deconstructing the Rainbow Warrior

In my game (and yours, reader) it was always the Frogmen
had clever theories. We did the dirty work

using the English language like a roguish trowel.
Tonight, two rubberised heads have set their Zodiac on course

from Okahu Bay. Past the Container port,
around Marsden Wharf, they're ferrying a transitive verb

called Bomb. In a hired campervan a man and a woman
smoke, check their watches, and bicker.

Turenges don't make it right, and anyway
the name is false, like their Swiss passports.

Half of Auckland, Dominique argues, has taken their number.
She's exaggerating of course. He refuses to panic.

A beautiful night. You can see the lighthouse light
on off Rangitoto, and an undercover moon

casual among clouds over North Head. Here come
the rubber boys back in their puttering Zodiac.

Remember, reader, poems don't deal in fact —
this is all a bad dream in the Élysée Palace.

Now scatter — it goes like the Paris Metro, according to plan.
Soon you will hear explosions. Someone will die.

More than a ship will founder. And the theory? Ah, the theory!
Dig a hole for it with your English trowels.

J. C. Sturm

HONESTLY

for Jim

It's all very well for you,
Safe and smug on the other side,
Knowing at last without doubt
All the answers you spent
Your whole life looking for
With not much more success
Than Frame, McCahon
Johnson at his best.

All very well for you,
But how about me
Still stranded in the garden,
Wide awake now and all ears
Needing to be told,
I mean, desperately needing
To be told what it's all about
And where to go from here.

You cannot hold out on me
This time. I know you know.
Tell you what — send me
An unmistakable sign
Pointing the right direction,
One omnipotent, omniscient
Syllable explaining all,

And I will try to forget
(Much harder than forgiving)
All the lies and deception
You brought to our living.

After all, they never made
Much difference, did they?

Robert Sullivan

Listen to the Rhythm of the Falling Rain

You, her and him, are in this —
it is a jug of pure water in the likeness
of a virgin glazed with rain beside white
chickens, or a mountain pinned to a railway

station (an installation), and in this way
the rain courses through holies, idols,
people of pain and passion, chance rain
that bends heads with its drops, dissolves,

shatters light, carries logs in bending streams.
Men and women scramble to dam the wondrous rain.
They cannot understand its massive rhythm:
that such a cascade feeds on joy and not

on competition. It is grace that sets
sun moon and stars to shine. Laughter
comes from talking, pain from healing.
Rain moves the strongest hearts.

Apirana Taylor

Sad Joke on a Marae

Tihei Mauriora I called
Kupe Paikea Te Kooti
Rewi and Te Rauparaha.
I saw them
grim death and wooden ghosts
carved on the meeting house wall.

In the only Maori I knew
I called
Tihei Mauriora.
Above me the tekoteko raged.
He ripped his tongue from his mouth
and threw it at my feet.

Then I spoke.
My name is Tu the freezing worker.
Ngati D.B. is my tribe.
The pub is my Marae.
My fist is my taiaha.
Jail is my home.

Tihei Mauriora I cried.
They understood
the tekoteko and the ghosts
though I said nothing but
Tihei Mauriora
for that's all I knew.

Charlotte Trevella

The Red Dress

The soil is swollen
with them, toadstools; scarlet
and scabby-mouthed,
bubbling under the pines.

There will be frost soon
and so many dresses to mend.

Some things are left unsaid.
There is the clock-work
mouse, the flowers on the
table, the doll with no arms,
the red dress.

How she wore it
that morning
and you hated the colour,
like a sore,
like a scarab.
How the hair you
plaited unravelled in
someone else's hand.

Stop searching.
What would you do
with the body, sew it
shut with roses, hang it
to billow with her dresses
on the line?

There will be frost soon
and at night something
even bigger will clatter
at your bedside,
like scissors,
like the sewing machine
with no thread left.

Chris Tse

In Which the Author Interviews a Dead Man

No one ever asked me to speak, or took the time to fill a moment with my presence. We cannot hide from ourselves in the dark. I crouch down in the damp void and listen as they pass words about me between themselves like borrowed scandal. The loudest, hungriest voices drown out all reason.

Yes, people talk, talk, talk and say such pointless things. And now, when talking is what will anchor me in their thoughts, such economy of blame will lead us nowhere. They risk my fate of leaving this world nameless.

For years I lit incense and prayed for my share of good fortune, holding fast to the belief that patience brings luck to those who traverse life's terrain with humble expectation. Now such a dispensation numbs me.

I often thought about the things I left behind, how the distance that once indulged me slowly smothered the dreams of those I made promises to. How my wife waited, how my bad luck clung to me like a wandering ghost. We are all losers in a stoic game. Unkind or unsettled, it made no difference in the long run; I took it all like a prized fool.

There is night fading into view with its hoard of loaded pauses, each intake of breath an assertion of my dues. Some stillness makes its way into death's song; some strange madness cocoons me. I suppose having seen their worst at work this may very well be a good year to fade away.

If I'm to acknowledge *him*, his part in my current state, then I can only say that he might've done it sooner, that if our paths had crossed on any other day or in any other street the outcome would be no different. I'd still be face down in the dirt and for a moment he'd be the bravest man.

And so are we now co-dependent — the scandal that holds the hand of the other? This intimate relationship begs to die a sure death, for there is no comfort in such a connection.

Brian Turner

Just This

'Find your place on the planet, dig in, and take responsibility from there.'
— Gary Snyder

Affecting without affectation, like the sere hills
then the early evening sky where Sirius dominates
for a time, then is joined by lesser lights,

stars indistinct as those seen through the canopies
of trees shaking in the wind. There's this wish
to feel part of something wholly explicable

and irreplaceable, something enduring
and wholesome that suppresses the urge to fight . . .
or is there? Ah, the cosmic questions

that keep on coming like shooting stars
and will, until, and then what? All I can say
is that for me nothing hurts more

than leaving and nothing less than coming home,
when a nor'wester's gusting in the pines
like operatic laughter, and the roadside grasses

are laced with the blue and orange and pink
of bugloss, poppies and yarrow, all of them
swishing, dancing, bending, as they do, as we do.

Hone Tuwhare
DEEP RIVER TALK

It's cold: it's golden; a magnificent
orange disc playing peek-a-boo
from the far-side of straggly
strings of leafless rastafarian willows
growing on the other side of the river.
The river's wide here: it's

undecided: it's steeling itself
never to turn and go back uphill.
Steam's rising from it and it's
not the early morning sun that's
doin' it; I can't raise heat
from the sun yet.

The veins of the river are swollen.
They're bending to the tide's
up-swing: tempers are like sails
shredding in a gale.

There's talk of a merger. A know-all
insect on stilts has just walked out
on top of the waters to supervise
the talks; I suppose pretending
to be Jesus.

In the sunlight mullet are jumpin'
and making lovin' archways of silver
for the migratory ocean-seeking eels
eeling their way down down; down
to the river-mouth and away.

The river's pushy, 'Back off! Thus far
and NO further —'

'I'll see YOU outside, mate,' says
the sea, turning. A swish, a tiny
whip and swirl of water —

Snap!

Daddy-long-legs has joined his
ancestors by way of a hungry trout's
stomach & stomach-ejector.

Happens to people too, nowadays — with
sharks hangin' around a lot.

Tim Upperton

KINDNESS

Evening light, olive oil poured
from a high jug: streaming over
the burnished back of the cricket
riding its bowing grass stem; glossing
the spade with its broken handle
leaning on the strainer-post that is itself
leaning, its crumbly lichen glowing,
the wire tired and slack; pooling
on the surface of the *leylandii* stump,
with its surround of buttery chips
from inexpert swipes of the axe.

Light is light, it is not kindness,
but if kindness had a colour, perhaps
it would be this — yes, you turn away
impatiently, yet it's you who cannot
bear to crush a snail; who once, in heavy
traffic, abandoned the car, and in tears
strode to a maimed pukeko that fluttered
beside the wide road; you who killed
that bird with a swing and a crack —

stay with me, as the light goes
from gold, to grey, to black.

Rae Varcoe

My Hairdresser

My hairdresser says his daughter is unwell

He says all year she has had colds, flu, pains and women's bothers

He says, after loads of tests, a diagnosis has been found

My hairdresser explains that the stomach is like a funnel

and all the food drops down onto a knobbly mat

The knobbles absorb calories and vitamins and iron

My hairdresser says his daughter has no knobbles on her mat

She now eschews gluten and takes iron through a drip

My hairdresser says she is no better

My hairdresser says his daughter is depressed

My hairdresser's wife does not agree with Citalopram

My hairdresser is paying for counselling

The mirror says my hairdresser has not been concentrating

Louise Wallace

I feel like I am having the world's heaviest baby

is what I say to Rory
about the book.
        He agrees.

Every day
it gets larger, and is harder
to carry with me. It seems
it will never be done.
        Rory bears

the weight too, mostly
on his thin lower legs.
At nights after work
he arrives home, flops
on the couch, and I rest
cold flannels
on his bulbous ankles
and one on his forehead
for the flush.
        From under

the flannel, feet higher
than his head, he screams
at a Mormon to get
the hell away.
        Him

and his goddamn dog.

Ian Wedde

To Art and Praxis

Kilometres of shining sand in which the blue sky's
Clouds wave, mean nothing. The waves,
Too, are meaningless. So are the mountains whose peaks
Are flushed with dawn, or dusk, depending on the time
Of day. Time also means nothing.

Out there in the wilderness where art and praxis
Have yet to tangle, time is just another
Neurosis. It's the Sublime that now approaches through
The mountain passes, along the shining strand,
And filled with awe and terror we sense how time

Diminishes us, making monumental the mountains
And the strand, the avalanches and the shipwrecks. But now Science
Begins to measure the avalanches and the shipwrecks, recording
The roars of both until they become the kind
Of music that will make the mall's ordinary crowd

Into a choir, and this random festoon of blooms
Into a memorial drenched with tears, and this shy
Sideways look into a great allegory of passion,
In which huge bronze bells ring dooms
Of unrequited love, great empires

Crash and burn, dynasties go phut,
And just when you thought you knew how this would end
Its meaning, too, eludes you. It doesn't
End — instead, a little, laconic tune,
Like someone merely whistling, fades away.

Albert Wendt

Last Night

Last night   all night   a blustery wind blew from the Ko'olau
It had no face and eyes and didn't know it had a tongue
Last night   all night   on the steep slopes of the valley
a dog barked as slippery as the pebbles of the Mānoa stream
that will never know it is alive and singing for the sea
The touch of my mother's fingers on my eyes kept me awake

In our house I needed to be afraid
I needed the healing of the blue darkness
that doesn't know it has desires
and my mother who wants my forgiveness
for having left fifty or so years ago
No one will be saved   I heard her say to a child
who needed to grow a soul that wanted saving

She also promised me the morning's dolphin light
the skip and dance of the incoming tide
the quick intelligence of the rain
She promised me amazement
enough to fill my pockets
enough to give away and create a life with
My pockets are almost empty now

Last night I wanted her to peel off her face and stretch it across mine
I wanted her to give me her tongue and eyes
I wanted her to promise she wouldn't die again without me

Last night   all night   she waited for me
at the edge of the blue darkness

Tom Weston

The Sadness of Gifts

A man saw his wife wrapped as a Christmas present.
The wind picked up their tent, slipping each guy-rope,
and bundled her away. In another instant she returned
to earth, the pivot on which she spun. The tent did not
consent to fly. The wind did not seek permission.
The man begged the wind to be gentle.

The wind was flagrant. It caught her hair and smashed
her down. It ran at yachts and cracked them like a whip
on their moorings. The man found his wife in the limp
wreckage of the tent. He heard the sea protest. He felt
twigs pull at his hair. He fumbled at zippers. The fabric
held tight, his broken Christmas present as if all life had
ebbed away. Still the wind tugged at them, urging him
to play.

A man saw his wife wrapped in wind. He was dashed
if he could remember anything more than that. There
were pegs in the ground. The ground had cheated him,
giving her leave to fly away. She had never thought
to fly. He cursed his thought of it, that dreams had
taught the wind this thing.

Pat White

Learning to Live Outdoors

Watch for the wing-beat
the pattern defines the breed, my old man said
duck shooting south of Ruatapu
you were at home . . . much as anywhere
in that lagoon of flax, salt wind
back of the beach where eels stirred
mud, unable to turn your poacher's back
on the banks of the Totara river, trout
there for the tickling

I pestered your shadow with my feet
your silence with questions

two or three years ago you told me
hawthorn is good firewood, we even
burned it green, Dad and me
that was the last, next time I called
you sat with eyes closed, pattern of flight
unknown, the bird as it were
had flown.

Alison Wong

THERE'S ALWAYS THINGS TO COME BACK TO THE KITCHEN FOR

a bowl of plain steamed rice
a piece of bitter dark chocolate
a slice of crisp peeled pear

a mother or father who understands
the kitchen is the centre of the universe

children who sail out on long elliptical orbits
and always come back, sometimes like comets, sometimes like moons

Sue Wootton

Alpine

Planning my return, with a mouthful
of snow. How I might talk

with it, merely, or else let you sip
off my tongue

tussock-filtered frozen altitude
in melt

just to watch your eyes widen, then close,
taste buds

locating the exact peak, its height, which storm,
each crystal's

complicated individuality, how it dropped
particularly here and

sea-level, salt-mingled now. One mouthful
of deliquescing snow

to alter our ridgeline lips. How, frisson-
caped, we might kiss.

Sonja Yelich

WIRES

Here is the radio from the *inside out* with mechanics.
Who brings me stories of accents lost from nations
whose nationals don't vote.
Where a roadmap is spin for not sure.
These are the valves of ceos verging on perjury.
& those are the wires of pharmac & farmers
whose codes *trick*.
Beef is an infection.
& war is a 30 second commercial
made in the Philippines from fingers of kids.
These are the times when buying
is Branding & Dreaming is paying or not.
With *Nero burning Rom off.*
& that is the tube who passes the story
to the heart of my ear. *From Radiowood.*
With the lure of Free True News.

Ashleigh Young

Doors

Down the hallway, there are no skylights
and the wallpaper is so tangled a wilderness even the trees
are lost, and all the young girls, their parents,
their faithful dogs. I search for them here,
each of my family.

Behind one door my mother springs back like a trap,
her arms opened up
to consume me.

A high wind rackets through the hallway
bursting open another —
it is my brother, with hands fisted on hips
standing tall in red sneakers on Christmas day
his eyes narrowed to meet mine;
he is a man in a cape, billowing, ready to fly.

Doors open one after the other
upon my eldest brother,
who holds each like a person's shoulder
or a shield
that he lowers slowly away from his body,
and in each doorway he is older.

Behind sliding doors I find my father.
He steps backward into a windowless room,
looking not at me but patiently over the top of my head,
as if counting the beats of a pulse:
I am not in an elevator

but he is so sure, I believe him when he tells me
that I've stopped on the wrong floor.
After all, I have not taken this way home before —

the geography of my family is unfamiliar.

Karen Zelas

Small Islands of Difference

night has stolen the day

slipped luminous
mother-of-pearl in its pocket

the tide sucks slap on the breakwater
strangers black against black

white last light from a line of
foam gleams on

the white of eye, the lift of brow
a greeting

turtles that pass
in the evening

a guitar, a bare bulb
harmony, small islands

of light. we live
in the shadows

understanding is
all, encompasses

all you could name:
charts, journals, the sextant

to navigate difference
let us sit side by side

here
on fine pandana matting

Poet Biographies

Fleur Adcock (1934–) lives in England but was born in New Zealand, where she spent her teenage years and early adulthood. Adcock has published numerous collections of poetry, and edited several, including *The Faber Book of Twentieth Century Women's Poetry* (1987), and translated the work of two Romanian poets and a Latin collection of verse. She was made an OBE in 1996 and a Companion of the New Zealand Order of Merit (CNZM) in 2008.

Johanna Aitchison (1972–) was born in the Bay of Islands and now lives in Palmerston North, where she is a lecturer at International Pacific College. She is a qualified lawyer and schoolteacher, and has an MA in Creative Writing. Her second volume of poems, *A Long Girl Ago* (VUP) was a finalist in the Montana New Zealand Book Awards 2007, and her work was anthologised in *The Best of Best New Zealand Poems* (VUP, 2011). 'Letters from Japanese Kids' is a found poem comprised of excerpts of letters from children she taught while on the JET Programme in Hokkaido, Japan.

Raewyn Alexander (1955–) is a fourth generation New Zealander of French, Irish, English and Scots descent. Born in Hamilton, she has travelled widely and now lives in Grey Lynn, Auckland. A narrative writing lecturer at Unitec, her novels, poetry, stories and writing in other media have been published in New Zealand, Australia and the USA. An imaginary memoir, *Glam Rock Boyfriends*, is due in 2014, as is another poetry collection, *Our Mother Flew Unassisted* (both from Brightspark Books).

John Allison (1950–) was born in Blenheim, and was fortunate to see much of New Zealand during his childhood, following his surveyor father as his chainman and thus learning the lie of the land. His poems have been published in numerous journals worldwide. He was the featured poet in *Poetry New Zealand* 14, and is the author of four books of poetry. His book on perception, imagination and poetry, *A Way of Seeing*, was published in 2003 by Lindisfarne Press in the USA. 'Near Death Experience' was first published in *Both Roads Taken* (Sudden Valley Press, 1997), and subsequently collected in *Balance: New and Selected Poems* (Five Islands Press, 2006).

Nick Ascroft (1973–) grew up in Oamaru and Te Anau, before listing to Dunedin like a drunken tug boat. He has published two collections of poetry, *From the Author of* (VUP, 2000) and *Nonsense* (VUP, 2003). He has lived in the UK since 2007 and currently works for Bloomsbury Publishing.

Tusiata Avia (1966–) has published two books of poetry, *Wild Dogs Under My Skirt* (VUP, 2004) and *Bloodclot* (VUP, 2009), and two children's books, *Mele and the Fofo* and *The Song*. Known for her dynamic performance style, she has also written and performed a one-woman poetry show, also called *Wild Dogs Under My Skirt*, that toured on and off from 2002 to 2008 in places as diverse as Moscow, Jerusalem and Vienna, as well as destinations closer to home. Avia has held a number of residencies, including the Fulbright Pacific Writer's Fellowship at the University of Hawai'i and the Ursula Bethell Writer in Residence at the University of Canterbury. She is regularly published in international literary journals and invited to appear at writers festivals around the globe. In 2013, Avia was the recipient of the Janet Frame Literary Trust Award. In 2014 she travelled to Philadelphia to perform for Phantom at the New Hope Arts Centre.

Stu Bagby (1947–) was born in Te Kopuru, near Dargaville. His last paid job was as a gravedigger at the Schnapper Rock Road cemetery on Auckland's North Shore. These days he spends most of his time cultivating vegetables and maintaining a very large garden on his block of land near Albany, north of Auckland. He also writes, reads a great deal of non-fiction — mainly literary biography — and judges the occasional poetry competition.

Hinemoana Baker (1968–) (Ngāti Raukawa, Ngāti Toa Rangatira, Te Āti Awa, Kāi Tahu, England, Germany) completed an MA in Creative Writing at Victoria University. Her first collection, *mātuhi | needle* (Perceval Press, 2004), was a New Zealand and American co-publication. Taki Rua Theatre produced two of her plays in the 1990s. Her poetry has appeared in a number of journals and anthologies, and she co-edited *Kaupapa: New Zealand Poets, World Issues*. She teaches creative writing online through Whitireia Community Polytechnic. Baker was the Stout Research Centre/Reader's Digest Fellow in 1998, the Arts Queensland poet-in-residence in 2009, and an Iowa University International Writing Program Fellow in 2010. She is writer-in-residence at Victoria University's International Institute of Modern Letters in 2014. Her third collection, *waha | mouth*, is to be published by Victoria University Press in 2014.

Serie Barford (1960–) was born in New Zealand. She is a performance poet of Samoan, Celtic, Scandinavian and Algonquin Indian ancestry. She has worked in community education and teaches literacy in a multicultural secondary school. Her latest poetry collection is entitled *Tapa Talk* (Huia, 2007), and she is currently revising a short story collection for publication.

Sarah Jane Barnett (1977–) is a writer, tutor and book reviewer who lives in Wellington. Her first collection of poems, *A Man Runs into a Woman*, was published by Hue & Cry Press in 2012, and was a finalist in the 2013 New Zealand Post Book Awards. Her work has appeared in various publications, including *Sport*, *Landfall*, *Best New Zealand Poems* and *Southerly*. She is currently completing a creative PhD in the field of Ecopoetics. She blogs at theredroom.org.

James K. Baxter (1926–1972) was born in Dunedin. Baxter completed university studies in Dunedin and teachers' college in Wellington, and undertook numerous jobs. He was a prolific writer of essays, critical work, social commentary, fiction, plays, children's poems (collected in *The Tree House and other poems for children*, Price Milburn, 1974) and poetry collections. Baxter was part of the Wellington Group (including W. H. Oliver, Louis Johnston and Alistair Te Ariki Campbell). He was the Burns Fellow at the University of Otago from 1966 to 1967, and was married to the poet J. C. Sturm. In the final years of his life he established a commune at Jerusalem, on the Whanganui River.

David Beach (1959–) has lived mostly in Wellington, the main exception being 16 years in Sydney from 1986 to 2002. His previous writing includes work as a chess columnist, film reviewer, and for the Department of Education's primary school news bulletins. He has published three collections of sonnets with Victoria University Press, the latest being *Scenery and Agriculture* (2012).

Tony Beyer (1948–) was born in Auckland, where he currently lives. For over 40 years he has had parallel careers in poetry and secondary school teaching. Married since 1970, he and his wife Mandy have two adult children and three grandchildren. His most recent books are *Dream Boat: Selected Poems* (HeadworX, 2007) and *Great South Road and South Side*, two longer poems (Puriri Press, 2013). 'Cut Lilac' was first published in *Comment*, September 1980, and subsequently in *Dancing Bear* (Melaleuca Press, 1981); this is its ninth appearance in print.

PETER BLAND (1934–) was born in the UK. He is both a writer and an actor, and has published plays, several volumes of poetry, several children's books and a memoir. He was a founding member of Downstage Theatre in Wellington, and has moved between England and New Zealand throughout his life. His latest book is *Breath Dances* (Steele Roberts, 2013).

JENNY BORNHOLDT (1960–) was born in Lower Hutt. She has published numerous collections of poetry, the most recent of which is *The Hill of Wool* (VUP, 2011). Her collection *The Rocky Shore* (VUP, 2008) won the Montana New Zealand Book Award in 2009. Bornholdt has edited various anthologies with her husband and fellow poet, Gregory O'Brien, including *An Anthology of New Zealand Poetry in English* (Oxford University Press, 1998) and *My Heart Goes Swimming: New Zealand Love Poems* (Random House, 2000). She was awarded the Katherine Mansfield Memorial Fellowship in 2002, an Arts Foundation Laureate Award in 2003, was the Te Mata Estate Poet Laureate from 2005 to 2007 and the Victoria University writer-in-residence in 2010.

CHARLES BRASCH (1909–1973) was born in Dunedin. He published six volumes of poetry (one appearing posthumously), and made a significant contribution to arts and letters in New Zealand as the founder in 1947 of the literary journal *Landfall*, which he edited for 20 years. Brasch was a generous patron of artists such as Colin McCahon and Toss Woollaston, and was instrumental in establishing fellowships for writers and artists at the University of Otago. He left his literary and personal papers to the university's Hocken Collections; this archive was recently accorded UNESCO 'Memory of the World' status. Brasch's *Journals 1938–1945* were published in 2013 by Otago University Press.

DIANA BRIDGE (1942–) is a Wellington poet who has published five collections of poems with Auckland University Press. The latest of these is *Aloe and Other Poems* (2009). In 2010 she was awarded the Lauris Edmond Memorial Award for distinguished contribution to New Zealand poetry. She is among the poets whose work has recently been added to the UK Poetry Archive. Bridge, who has a PhD in Classical Chinese Poetry, has worked on the China-based poems of Robin Hyde, and an essay on Hyde, 'O To Be a Dragon', was published in the *New Zealand Journal of Asian Studies* (June 2008). She is currently collaborating on a translated selection of classical Chinese poems.

Bub Bridger (1924–2009) was a poet, actor and short story writer of Māori, Irish and English ancestry. She began writing at the age of 50, after attending a writers' workshop run by the late historian Michael King at Victoria University. Her writing was widely anthologised and she published several poetry collections. She also wrote for television and broadcast radio.

Sarah Broom (1972–2013) was a New Zealand poet and scholar. Born and educated in the South Island, she studied in the UK at the University of Leeds, where she was awarded an MA in English. She later gained a DPhil from Oxford University. She was a lecturer at Somerville College, Oxford, before returning in 2000 to New Zealand, where she held a post-doctoral fellowship at Massey University (Albany) and lectured in English at the University of Otago. Her book *Contemporary British and Irish Poetry: An Introduction* (Palgrave Macmillan) was published in 2006, followed by two books of poetry: *Tigers at Awhitu* (AUP/ Carcanet, 2010) and the posthumous collection *Gleam* (AUP, 2013).

Amy Brown (1984–) teaches creative writing at the University of Melbourne. Her first collection of poetry, *The Propaganda Poster Girl* (VUP, 2008), was shortlisted for the New Zealand Book Awards in 2009. Her second poetry book, a contemporary epic titled *The Odour of Sanctity*, was published by Victoria University Press in 2013.

Diane Brown (1951–) is a novelist, memoirist and poet who runs a creative writing school, Creative Writing Otago, in Dunedin. Her publications include two collections of poetry, *Before the Divorce We Go to Disneyland* (Tandem Press, 1997), which won the NZSA Best First Book of Poetry at the Montana New Zealand Book Awards in 1997, and *Learning to Lie Together* (Godwit, 2004); two novels, including *Eight Stages of Grace* (Random House, 2002), which was a finalist in the Montana New Zealand Book Awards 2003; a travel memoir; and a further prose/poetic work, *Here Comes Another Vital Moment* (Random House, 2006). She won the Janet Frame Memorial Award in 2012 and a Beatson Fellowship in 2013. Also in that year she was made a Member of the New Zealand Order of Merit for services to writing and education.

James Brown (1966–) published his latest poetry collection, *Warm Auditorium* (VUP), in 2012. He is the author behind the useful non-fiction booklet *Instructions for Poetry Readings* (Braunias University Press, 2005) and edited *The Nature of Things: Poems from the New Zealand Landscape* (Craig Potton, 2005). He teaches the poetry writing workshop at the

International Institute of Modern Letters at Victoria University, and is part of the writing team at the Museum of New Zealand Te Papa Tongarewa.

Owen Bullock (1967–) wanted to be a writer since he was ten years old. He made a start with short stories and has been writing poetry and songs since his teens. He has been a regular contributor to New Zealand journals, including *takahē*, *Sport*, *Landfall* and *Poetry New Zealand*, and has edited *Poetry New Zealand*, *Bravado*, *Spin* and *Kokako*. He is well known as a haiku poet and in 2009 published his first haiku collection, *Wild Camomile* (Post Pressed). In 2010 he published a novella, *A Cornish Story* (Palores Publications).

Rachel Bush (1941–) was raised in Hawera. She now lives in Nelson where she taught for 19 years. Her most recent book is *Nice Pretty Things and Others* (VUP, 2011). Her work has been anthologised both in New Zealand and overseas.

Kate Camp (1972–) lives in Wellington. She is the author of five collections of poetry published by Victoria University Press: *Unfamiliar Legends of the Stars* (winner of Best First Book of Poetry at the Montana New Zealand Book Awards 1999), *Realia* (2001), *Beauty Sleep* (2005), *The Mirror of Simple Annihilated Souls* (winner of the New Zealand Post Book Award for Poetry 2011) and *Snow White's Coffin* (2013). The latter was written while Camp held the Creative New Zealand Berlin Writers' Residency, and was shortlisted for the New Zealand Post Book Awards in 2013. For over a decade Camp has been the voice of Kate's Klassics, conversations about classic literature with Radio New Zealand's Kim Hill. A collection of essays on classic books, also titled *Kate's Klassics*, was published by Penguin in 2005.

Alistair Te Ariki Campbell (1925–2009) was of Cook Islands and European descent. He spent his first seven years in the Cook Islands, and after his father's death moved to Dunedin. He graduated from Victoria University College and Wellington Teachers' College, and was an editor of the *School Journal* from 1955 to 1972. A poet and a novelist, with a prolific publishing record, Campbell received many honours, including a New Zealand Book Award for Poetry in 1982 and an honorary doctorate from Victoria University. In 2005 he received the Prime Minister's Award for Literary Achievement in Poetry and was made an Officer of the New Zealand Order of Merit (ONZM). He was married first to Fleur Adcock, and subsequently to Meg Andersen (Campbell).

Meg Campbell (1937–2007) was born and raised in Palmerston North and began to write in her forties. She published several collections of poetry and her writing appeared in a range of literary journals and magazines. She was married to the poet Alistair Te Ariki Campbell and lived on the Kapiti Coast.

Gordon Challis (1932–) was born into a family of Welsh origin, but spent very little time in that country due to his father's job as a technician with the BBC, based in London and Birmingham. The many switches of schools and homes had a highly unsettling effect and he became a school dropout. In later life, having emigrated to New Zealand in 1954, Challis completed training as a psychologist and social worker. Challis worked in psychiatric facilities in Porirua, Hastings and Canberra. He retired in 1988 and now lives in Golden Bay with his wife, Penny.

Janet Charman (1954–) grew up in the Hutt Valley and Taranaki and has worked as a nurse, university tutor, telephone operator and secondary school teacher. She graduated from the University of Auckland with an MA in English Literature. Charman was the 1997 University of Auckland Literary Fellow, and her collection of poems, *Cold Snack* (AUP, 2007), won the Montana New Zealand Book Award for Poetry in 2008. She has published seven volumes of poetry, most recently *At the White Coast* (AUP, 2012), a memoir of a year in Europe during the Thatcher era.

Geoff Cochrane (1951–) lives in Wellington. In addition to novels and short fiction, he has published many books of poetry, including *Pocket Edition* (VUP, 2009) and *The Worm in the Tequila* (VUP, 2010).

Glenn Colquhoun (1964–) is a poet and a doctor. He grew up in South Auckland and now works as a GP on the Kapiti Coast. His first book, *The Art of Walking Upright* (Steele Roberts, 1999), won the NZSA Jessie Mackay Award for Best First Book of Poetry in 2000. His third collection, *Playing God* (Steele Roberts, 2002), won the Montana New Zealand Book Award for Poetry in 2003. It has gone on to achieve the rare poetry feat of platinum sales. Colquhoun won the Glenn Schaeffer Prize in Modern Letters in 2004, and his latest collection, *North South* (Steele Roberts, 2009), was brought to life on stage with musical accompaniment at the Going West Books and Writers Festival. He has also published several books for children.

Kay McKenzie Cooke (1953–) lives in Dunedin and has published two books of poems. Her first, *Feeding the Dogs* (OUP, 2002), won the NZSA Jessie Mackay Award for Best First Book of Poetry at the 2003 Montana New Zealand Book Awards. Her third book, *Born to a Red-headed Woman*, will be published in 2014.

Allen Curnow (1911–2001) was born in Timaru and educated in Auckland and Canterbury. After studying for the Anglican ministry he turned to journalism, and from 1951 to 1976 he taught in the English Department at the University of Auckland. He received a DLitt from the University of Auckland. Curnow published numerous volumes of poems, seven of which (including his final collection, *The Bells of Saint Babel's*, AUP, 2001) won the New Zealand Book Award for Poetry. He also edited two anthologies of New Zealand verse, including the influential *Book of New Zealand Verse* (Caxton, 1945), and published critical essays and plays for radio and the stage. During his last decade his new work was almost exclusively first published in the *London Review of Books*. His many honours included honorary degrees from the universities of Auckland and Canterbury, the Commonwealth Poetry Prize (1988), the Queen's Gold Medal for Poetry (1989), the ONZ (1990) and the Cholmondeley Award for Poetry (1992). He was awarded the A. W. Reed Lifetime Achievement Award in 2000. In 2001, Curnow was the first poet commissioned to read work for the recently established Poetry Archive in Cambridge initiated by the Poet Laureate. He completed the recording of 17 poems two weeks before his death.

Ruth Dallas (1919–2008) was born in Invercargill. She published numerous collections of poetry as well as eight novels for children. Her fifth collection, *Walking on the Snow* (Caxton, 1976), received a New Zealand Book Award in 1977. Dallas worked with Charles Brasch at *Landfall*, and the University of Otago awarded her the Burns Fellowship and, a decade later, an Honorary Doctorate of Literature. She was made a CBE for her services to literature in 1989.

Lynn Davidson (1959–) writes fiction, poetry and essays. Her work has appeared in journals including *Sport* and *PN Review* and been broadcast on Radio New Zealand. She has published several collections of poetry, a novel — *Ghost Net* (OUP, 2003) — and a novella — *The Desert Road* (Rose Mira Books, 2014). In September 2013, Davidson had a writing fellowship at Hawthorden Castle in Scotland. She works as an educator and tutors students in short fiction and poetry.

Stephanie de Montalk (1945–) won the NZSA Jessie Mackay Award for Best First Book of Poetry in 2001 with her collection *Animals Indoors* (VUP, 2000); three further collections followed in 2002, 2005 and 2009. Her memoir/biography, *Unquiet World* (VUP), was published in 2001 and her historical novel, *The Fountain of Tears* (VUP), in 2006. De Montalk was writer-in-residence at Victoria University in 2005. In 2013 she completed a PhD in Creative Writing, the dissertation of which looks at chronic pain and will be published by Victoria University Press in 2014.

John Dickson (1944–) was born in Milton, South Otago. He was the Burns Fellow at the University of Otago in 1988 and the University of Waikato writer-in-residence in 2000. His latest publication is a CD called *Plain Song*, which was released in 2009. He currently lives in Christchurch.

Emily Dobson (1981–) is the author of *A Box of Bees* (VUP, 2005). She has an MA in Creative Writing from Victoria University, and was the Schaeffer Fellow to the Writers' Workshop at the University of Iowa from 2005 to 2006. She has worked as a singing teacher, life model and postie. She lives in rural Hawke's Bay with her husband and two children.

Lauris Edmond (1924–2000) grew up in Greenmeadows, Hawke's Bay, lived in rural New Zealand as an adult, and published her first collection of poetry when she was 51. Edmond published 17 volumes of poetry. She received many awards, including the PEN Best First Book Award for Poetry in 1975 for *In Middle Air* (Pegasus Press, 1975). Edmond was awarded the Katherine Mansfield Memorial Fellowship in 1981 and the Commonwealth Poetry Prize in 1985. She was made an OBE in 1986, won the Lilian Ida Smith Award for Poetry in 1987, and was awarded an honorary Doctorate of Literature from Massey University in 1988. She received the A. W. Reed Award for contribution to New Zealand literature in 1999. She wrote short stories, a novel, and radio and stage plays, and edited several books, including a volume of A. R. D. Fairburn's letters. Edmond was a founder of the review quarterly *New Zealand Books* and frequently contributed reviews and articles. She edited *New Zealand Love Poems: An Oxford Anthology* (2000) and co-edited *Essential New Zealand Poems* with Bill Sewell (Godwit, 2001).

Murray Edmond (1949–) is a poet, playwright, critic, dramaturge, editor, and Associate Professor in Drama at the University of Auckland. His recent publications include *Noh Business* (Atelos, 2005), *Walls to Kick and Hills to Sing From* (AUP, 2010), *Three Travels* (Holloway Press, 2012), dramaturgy for Indian Ink's *The Guru of Chai* (2010) and *Kiss the Fish* (2013), and issues 11 (2012) and 12 (2013) of the online journal *Ka Mate Ka Ora: A New Zealand Journal of Poetry and Poetics*, of which he is editor. A volume of critical writings, *Then It Was Now Again*, is forthcoming from Titus Books in 2014.

David Eggleton (1952–) was born in Auckland, grew up in both Fiji and New Zealand, and is part Polynesian. Eggleton has published a number of poetry collections, books of prose (on art, photography and pop music) and edited two anthologies. *South Pacific Sunrise* (Penguin, 1986) was co-winner of the PEN Best First Book of Poetry Award in 1987. He has travelled extensively as a performance poet and was named London's *Time Out* Street Entertainer of the Year for Poetry in 1985. Eggleton won the inaugural Book Reviewer of the Year Award in 1991, went on to win the same award five more times, and was shortlisted on seven other occasions. He has made award-winning short films and released several collaborative CDs of his work. He was the 1990 Burns Fellow at the University of Otago.

Riemke Ensing (1939–) was born in the Netherlands and has lived in New Zealand since 1951. She edited the first anthology of New Zealand women poets, *Private Gardens* (Caveman Books, 1977), and has published numerous collections of her own poetry, including *Talking Pictures: Selected Poems* (HeadworX, 2000). She was the Buddle Findlay Sargeson Fellow in 2002. Ensing won the NZSA Kevin Ireland Poetry Award in 2012, and in that same year was the recipient of the Lauris Edmond Memorial Award for Poetry.

Rangi Faith (1949–) was born in Timaru. He is a poet, anthologist and reviewer who has been widely published in New Zealand and overseas. He was first published in *Te Ao Hou* and substantially represented in *Into the World of Light* (Heinemann, 1982). He is the author of *Unfinished Crossword* (Hazard Press, 1990), *Rivers Without Eels* (Huia, 2001), and *Conversation With a Moahunter* (Steele Roberts, 2005). He also edited *Dangerous Landscapes* (Longman Paul, 1994), a collection of poetry for secondary school students. Presently writing at his home in Rangiora, he has recently retired from teaching and is currently preparing a new book for publication.

Fiona Farrell (1947–) was born in Oamaru and educated at Otago and Toronto universities (MPhil Drama). She has published several plays, including *Chook Chook*, one of Playmarket New Zealand's most popular scripts. She has also published two collections of short stories and six novels, several of which were shortlisted for the New Zealand Book Awards, beginning with her first novel, *The Skinny Louie Book* (Penguin, 1992), which won the New Zealand Book Award for Fiction in 1992. Four of her novels have also been nominated for the International IMPAC Dublin Award. She has published three collections of poetry, and her poems have appeared in many major anthologies. Her non-fiction includes a book of essays, *The Broken Book* (AUP, 2011), written following the Christchurch earthquakes. Her awards include the Menton Mansfield Fellowship in 1995, the Prime Minister's Award for Literary Achievement in 2007, and the ONZM for services to literature in 2011.

Cliff Fell (1955–) was born in London to an English mother and New Zealand father. His first poetry collection, *The Adulterer's Bible* (VUP, 2003), was awarded the NZSA Jessie Mackay Award for Best First Book of Poetry in 2004. A second collection, *Beauty of the Badlands* (VUP), was published in 2008.

Jan FitzGerald (1950–) was first noticed and admired as a poet by James K. Baxter and Hone Tuwhare, when she was a college student in the 1960s. In the 1970s, while working as a primary school teacher, she continued to write, spending weekends in Auckland with Tuwhare and reading alongside Baxter at his insistence. FitzGerald's work has appeared regularly in *Landfall*, *Arena* and *Mate*. Her first collection, *Strange Owls*, was published by Outrigger Press in 1978. Her second collection, *Flying Against the Arrow* (Wolfdale Press), was published in 2005, and Steele Roberts published her third collection, *On a Day Like This*, in 2010. FitzGerald is a full-time artist, and lives with her poet-painter husband, Leonard Lambert, in Napier.

Joan Fleming (1984–) completed an MA in Creative Writing at Victoria University in 2007. She was awarded the Biggs Poetry Prize, and edited *Turbine* that year. A chapbook of her prose poems, *Two Dreams in Which Things Are Taken*, was published by the DUETS project in 2010, and her debut collection of poetry, *The Same as Yes*, by Victoria University Press in 2011. In 2013 she completed an MA in Iterative Poetics at the University of Otago. Fleming has worked as an editor, copy writer, corporate communications advisor, nanny, waitress, barista, and teacher, and is currently pursuing a PhD in Ethnopoetics at Monash University, Melbourne.

Janet Frame (1924–2004) was born in Dunedin and educated at Waitaki Girls' High School. She completed teacher training in Dunedin and studied at the University of Otago. She published 20 works of fiction, poetry and non-fiction in her lifetime, winning many book awards across all categories. Another seven titles have been released posthumously. Her writing continues to be published, translated and critically acclaimed worldwide. She received numerous accolades in New Zealand and internationally, including two honorary doctorates, the Commonwealth Prize for Literature, and honorary membership of the American Academy of Arts and Letters. She was appointed CBE for services to literature in 1983, and made a member of the Order of New Zealand in 1990. She held several scholarships and residencies including the Burns, Mansfield and Sargeson fellowships. Her first poetry volume, *The Pocket Mirror* (George Braziller, 1967), earned the New Zealand Literary Fund Award for Achievement in 1969, and her second (posthumous) collection, *The Goose Bath* (Vintage, 2007), won the Montana New Zealand Book Award for Poetry.

Janis Freegard (1963–) was born in South Shields, England, and lived in South Africa and Australia before settling in New Zealand when she was 12. She is the author of *The Continuing Adventures of Alice Spider* (Anomalous Press, 2013) and *Kingdom Animalia: The Escapades of Linnaeus* (AUP, 2011), and co-author of *AUP New Poets 3* (2008). She also writes fiction and is a past winner of the BNZ Katherine Mansfield Award. Her poetry and short stories have been widely published in journals and anthologies. She lives in Wellington and blogs at janisfreegard.com.

Anne French (1956–) was born in Wellington and graduated from Victoria University with an MA. French became the managing editor of Oxford University Press (New Zealand), and moved to a similar position at the Museum of New Zealand Te Papa Tongarewa. She has published six volumes of poetry, with her first collection, *All Cretans Are Liars* (AUP, 1987), winning both the PEN Best First Book of Poetry Award and the New Zealand Book Award for Poetry in 1988. She was the inaugural writer-in-residence at Massey University in 1993.

Rhian Gallagher (1961–) was born in Timaru. She completed a BA at London University and a Postgraduate Diploma in Printing and Publishing at the London School of Printing. Her first collection, *Salt Water Creek* (Enitharmon Press, 2003), was shortlisted for the Forward Prize for First Collection. She received the Janet Frame Literary Trust Award in 2008 and her second collection, *Shift* (AUP, 2011), won the New Zealand Post Book Award for Poetry in 2012.

Denis Glover (1912–1980) was born in Dunedin, grew up in New Plymouth, went to Auckland Grammar School and graduated from Canterbury University College with a BA in English and Greek. Glover worked as a poet, printer, publisher and satirist. He established the Caxton Press in 1935, publishing collections by A. R. D. Fairburn, R. A. K. Mason and Allen Curnow. Glover published over 20 volumes of his own poetry, as well as prose books at various presses. He was the president of PEN and of the Friends of the Alexander Turnbull Library in the 1960s. He received an Honorary Doctorate of Literature from Victoria University in 1975.

Paula Green (1955–) was born in Auckland. She graduated from Wellington Teachers' College and from the University of Auckland (MA Honours, PhD Italian), and was the 2005 University of Auckland Literary Fellow. She has published eight poetry collections including several for children. She reviews poetry for the *New Zealand Herald* and visits schools regularly. The book she co-wrote with Harry Ricketts, *99 Ways into New Zealand Poetry* (Vintage, 2010), was shortlisted for the New Zealand Post Book Awards. In 2012 she edited *Dear Heart: 150 New Zealand Love Poems* (Godwit). Seraph Press published her latest collection of poems, *The Baker's Thumbprint*, in 2013. She runs two blogs: NZ Poetry Box, for children, and NZ Poetry Shelf, for adults and secondary school students. She recently edited *A Treasury of New Zealand Poetry for Children* (Random House, 2014) and her new children's collection, *The Letterbox Cat* (Scholastic), is forthcoming.

David Gregory (1949–) was born in England. He is a Christchurch-based poet and author of three books of poetry: *Always Arriving* and *Frame of Mind* (both Sudden Valley Press, 1997 and 1999), and more recently *Push* (Black Doris Press, 2008). He is also the co-editor of *Land Very Fertile: Banks Peninsula in Poetry and Prose* (CUP, 2008). His work has been published widely in New Zealand, USA and the UK. He is an active member of the Canterbury Poets Collective, and has been one of the editors of Sudden Valley Press.

Bernadette Hall (1945–) was born in Alexandra. She graduated with an MA (Honours) in Latin from the University of Otago, and until 2005 worked as a high school teacher in Dunedin and then in Christchurch. She was the Burns Fellow at the University of Otago in 1996, an Arts Fellow in the Artists in Antarctica Programme in 2004, the Victoria University writer-in-residence in 2006, and held the Rathcoola Residency in Ireland in 2007. She has edited several collections of poetry, including *Like Love Poems* (VUP, 2006), selected poems by Joanna Margaret Paul; the online anthology *Best New Zealand Poems* (VUP, 2011); and *The Judas Tree* (CUP, 2013), selected poems by Lorna Staveley Anker. Her most recent works are *The Lustre Jug* (VUP, 2009), a finalist in the 2010 New Zealand Post Book Awards, and *Life & Customs* (VUP, 2013).

Michael Harlow has published eight volumes of poems, including *Giotto's Elephant* (John McIndoe, 1992), which was shortlisted for the New Zealand Book Awards in 1992, and most recently *The Tram Conductor's Blue Cap* (AUP, 2009), which was a finalist in the New Zealand Book Awards in 2010. Associate and poetry editor at *Landfall* for ten years, he was the Katherine Mansfield Memorial Fellow in 1986, the Randell Cottage writer-in-residence in 2004, both the Burns Fellow and the inaugural Caselberg artist-in-residence in 2009, and the Wallace artist/writer-in-residence in 2011 and 2012. His *Selected Poems* was published by Cold Hub Press in 2014, and a volume of love poems, *Heart Absolutely I Can*, by Mākaro Press. His book *Take a Risk, Trust Your Language, Make a Poem* was awarded the PEN Best First Book of Prose in 1986. He lives and works as a writer, editor, and Jungian therapist in Central Otago.

Siobhan Harvey (1973–) is a poet and non-fiction author whose works include the poetry collections *Cloudboy* (OUP, 2014) and *Lost Relatives* (Steele Roberts, 2011), the work of literary criticism *Words Chosen Carefully: New Zealand Writers in Conversation* (Cape Catley, 2010), and the anthology *Our Own Kind: 100 New Zealand Poems about Animals* (Godwit, 2009). She is the winner of the 2013 Kathleen Grattan Poetry Award, and in 2012 was runner-up in both the Dorothy Porter Poetry Prize (Australia) and the Kevin Ireland Poetry Competition. The *Landfall* Essay Prize awarded her runner-up and highly commended in 2011 and 2013 respectively. Between 2006 and 2013 Harvey co-ordinated New Zealand's National Poetry Day. She has been a guest writer at literary festivals in Australia, Indonesia, the UK and New Zealand. She has a Poet's Page on the Poetry Archive (UK).

Dinah Hawken (1943–) was born in Hawera and now lives in Paekakariki on the Kapiti Coast. Her first book, *It Has No Sound and Is Blue* (VUP, 1987), won the 1987 Commonwealth Poetry Prize for Best First Time Published Poet. Of her six collections of poetry, four have been finalists in the New Zealand Book Awards, including her most recent book, *The Leaf-Ride* (VUP, 2011). She has also recently completed a collaborative book project, *page : stone : leaf*, with the stone sculptor John Edgar, published by Holloway Press.

Helen Heath (1970–) published her debut collection of poetry, *Graft*, with VUP in 2012 to critical acclaim. *Graft* won the NZSA Jessie Mackay Best First Book for Poetry Award in 2013 and was the first book of fiction or poetry to be shortlisted for the Royal Society of New Zealand Science Book Prize, also in 2013. Her poems, essays, articles and reviews have appeared in a range of journals and magazines in New Zealand, Australia, the UK and the USA. She is working toward her PhD in Creative Writing at Victoria University, exploring how science is represented in the work of post-war, contemporary UK poets writing at the turn of the millennium. She is using this research to write poems about the intersect between people and technology.

Jeffrey Paparoa Holman (1947–) emigrated to New Zealand from London with his family in 1950. He grew up mainly on the West Coast and has a PhD in Māori Studies from the University of Canterbury. He has published seven collections of poetry, including *As Big as a Father* (Steele Roberts, 2002), which was a finalist for the Montana New Zealand Book Awards in Poetry in 2003.

Ingrid Horrocks (1975–) writes poetry and creative non-fiction. She has a PhD from Princeton University and teaches creative writing at Massey University in Wellington. Her latest collection is *Mapping the Distance* (VUP, 2010).

John Horrocks (1943–) teaches psychology at the Wellington Institute of Technology. He spent 16 years farming north of Auckland and in the Wairarapa, before completing a doctorate on poetry and readers' imaginings.

David Howard (1959–) spent 35 years compiling one book: *The Incomplete Poems* (Cold Hub Press, 2011). He received the NZSA Mid-Career Writers' Award in 2009, the University of South Pacific Press Poetry Prize in 2011, and the University of Otago Burns Fellowship in 2013.

Keri Hulme (1947–) of Kai Tahu has had a close relationship with other life forms since early childhood (helped by extreme myopia). Also a novelist and short story writer, she gained international recognition with her novel *The Bone People* (Spiral, 1984), which won the Booker Prize, the Mobil Pegasus Award and the New Zealand Book Award for Fiction. Of Lancashire and Orkney Scots as well as Kai Tahu descent, she lives in an isolated area of the South Island.

Sam Hunt (1946–) was born at Castor Bay, on Auckland's North Shore. He attended St Peter's College, where the poet Ken Arvidson taught him in his final year. Hunt has published 15 collections of poems, the most recent being *Knucklebones: Poems 1962–2012* (Craig Potton, 2012). Hunt was a Burns Fellow in 1976, and in 1986 was awarded a QSM. In 2010 he was further honoured when he was made a Companion of the New Zealand Order of Merit (CNZM) for services to poetry. In 2012 he received the Prime Minister's Award for Literary Achievement in Poetry. He has a new collection — *Salt River Songs* — coming out wiith Craig Potton in 2014, and a second album with David Kilgour & the Heavy 8s — for which Hunt has provided the lyrics and lead vocals.

Jan Hutchison (1932–) was born in Petone, and started writing after her children grew up. She was a librarian for many years. She is interested in the environment, language and mythology. She has Māori and Pākehā grandchildren. Her most recent poetry collection is *The Happiness of Rain* (Steele Roberts, 2012). Her poems have been published in journals such as *Quadrant* and *JAAM*, and in various anthologies. She has been placed first in international poetry competitions held by *takahē* and another held by *Bravado*. She lives with her partner, Hamish, in Christchurch and is working on another collection of poetry.

Kevin Ireland (1933–) was born in Auckland as Kevin Jowsey. He has published numerous volumes of poetry, prose, non-fiction and an opera libretto. He co-founded the poetry journal *Mate* before moving to England for 25 years. Ireland was the second recipient of the Prime Minister's Award for Literary Achievement in Poetry and was made an OBE, both in 2004. He was the writer-in-residence at the University of Canterbury in 1986, the Sargeson Fellow in 1987, and the University of Auckland Literary Fellow in 1989. His memoir, *Under the Bridge and Over the Moon* (Vintage, 1998), won the history and biography section of the Montana New Zealand Book Awards in 1999, and *Literary*

Cartoons (Hurricane, 1977) won the New Zealand Book Award for Poetry. He has published two book-length essays, on how to fish and on getting old. He received the A. W. Reed Award for Contribution to New Zealand Literature in 2006.

ROB JACKAMAN (1945–) was born in Ipswich, England, and read English Literature at King's College, Cambridge. He won a Commonwealth Scholarship to the University of Auckland, and studied for a PhD under C. K. Stead. He was appointed a lecturer in English at the University of Canterbury in 1972, specialising in twentieth-century British and American poetry, contemporary Australian and New Zealand poetry, and Renaissance Literature. He also taught in the university's creative writing course. He is a widely published poet and a poetry editor, notably for Hazard Press.

ANNA JACKSON (1967–) is a poet, essayist, editor, and fiction and academic writer, with a DPhil from Oxford University. She has produced five volumes of poetry, and her work also appears in two collaborative collections. Born in Auckland, she now lives in Wellington, where she teaches at Victoria University. Her latest collection is entitled *Thicket* (AUP, 2011).

MICHAEL JACKSON (1940–) is the author of 30 books of poetry, ethnography and fiction. Since 1983 he has lived and worked abroad, but he returns to New Zealand every year to keep the home fires burning. He currently teaches at Harvard University.

HELEN JACOBS (1929–) was born in Patea. She came to live in Lowry Bay in 1954, and lived in Eastbourne for 36 years. Since 1984 six collections of her poetry have been published, the most recent being *Dried Figs* (Sudden Valley Press) in 2012. Her work has appeared in many magazines and anthologies, including *Yellow Pencils* (Oxford University Press, 1988), *Oxford Anthology of Love Poems* (2000), *Essential New Zealand Poems* (Godwit, 2001), *My Garden, My Paradise* (Hazard Press, 2003), *This Earth's Deep Breathing* (Godwit, 2007) and *Our Own Kind* (Godwit, 2009). Following community and environmental involvement, she was elected Mayor of Eastbourne in 1980 and appointed to the Planning Tribunal in 1986. Since retiring to Christchurch in 1994 she has been active in the poetry community and the Canterbury Poets Collective.

Adrienne Jansen (1947–) has published three novels, several non-fiction works and a collection of poetry. She also writes for children. She works as a writer at the Museum of New Zealand Te Papa Tongarewa and teaches writing at Whitireia Community Polytechnic.

Louis Johnson (1924–1988) was born in Wellington. He graduated from Wellington Teachers' College and, after teaching for several years, turned to journalism. Johnson established and edited the *New Zealand Poetry Yearbook* (1951–1964) and was associated with the Wellington Group. From 1963 he edited the *School Journal* as well as contributing to radio and television programmes and newspaper columns. In 1968 he left New Zealand to teach at Mitchell College of Advanced Education in Bathurst, NSW, returning in 1980 to become Victoria University Writing Fellow and president of PEN. A prolific poet, he was a generous supporter of other writers, now acknowledged in the annual Louis Johnson New Writers Award. He published over 14 poetry collections and held the Katherine Mansfield Memorial Fellowship at the time of his death.

Mike Johnson (1947–) lives on Waiheke Island. He has published five poetry collections and eight novels, including the award-winning *Dumb Show* (Longacre, 1996). He has won a number of awards and residencies, including the University of Auckland Literary Fellowship. His last novel was *Travesty* (Titus Books, 2010). He teaches creative writing at AUT University.

Andrew Johnston (1963–) was born in Upper Hutt. He has published five volumes of poetry, the first of which, *How to Talk* (VUP, 1993), won the 1994 New Zealand Book Award for Poetry. He edited *Moonlight: New Zealand Poems on Death and Dying* (Godwit, 2008) and with Robyn Marsack co-edited *Twenty Contemporary New Zealand Poets* (VUP/Carcanet, 2009). Since 1997 he has lived in France, where he worked as an editor for the *International Herald Tribune* for 11 years. He is now an editor and consultant for United Nations agencies and development groups.

Jan Kemp (1949–) has recently written *Voicetracks* (2012) and *Dante's Heaven* (2006), both from Puriri Press, Auckland. A bilingual edition, *Dantes Himmel*, was released in 2012 at the Frankfurt Book Fair. Kemp was project manager of '25 New Zealand Poets' for the UK Poetry Archive 2012, where her own work has been represented since 2006. She lives with her husband in Kronberg im Taunus outside Frankfurt am Main, where she writes and teaches EFL part-time. She still feels the strong pull of her familial and poetic roots, despite having become a 'New Zealand European'. Kemp is working on a manuscript, *Slippery Ice & the Love Planet*, hearing and writing poems first in either English or German, then translating the German.

ANNE KENNEDY (1959–) writes fiction, poetry and screenplays. Her most recent book is the novel *The Last Days of the National Costume* (Allen & Unwin, 2013). *The Darling North* (AUP, 2012) won the 2013 New Zealand Post Book Award for Poetry. She has also won the Montana New Zealand Book Award for Poetry, the BNZ Katherine Mansfield Short Story Award and has held fellowships at the University of Auckland and at the University of Hawai'i at Mānoa, where she taught fiction and screenwriting for a number of years. Kennedy is co-editor of *Ika* and the online arts journal *Trout*. She teaches screenwriting at the Manukau Institute of Technology. In July 2014 she took up the Michael King Writers' Fellowship at the University of Auckland.

FIONA KIDMAN (1940–) was born in Hawera and is a short story writer, novelist and poet. She has also worked as a librarian, a producer and a critic. Kidman has published about 30 books, including five poetry collections, of which the most recent, *Where Your Left Hand Rests* (Godwit, 2010), was published after a long break from writing poetry. Her awards include the A. W. Reed Lifetime Achievement Award at the Montana New Zealand Book Awards in 2001, the Katherine Mansfield Memorial Fellowship in Menton in 2006, and the Creative New Zealand Michael King Fellowship in 2008. In 1988 Kidman was made an OBE, and in 1998 named Dame Companion of the New Zealand Order of Merit, as well as (by France) a Chevalier de l'Ordre des Arts et des Lettres and a Chevalier of the French Legion of Honour in 1999. She is the President of Honour of the New Zealand Book Council.

KOENRAAD KUIPER (1944–) was born in Hanover, Germany, and emigrated to New Zealand in 1950. He is currently Professor Emeritus at the University of Canterbury and Adjunct Professor at the University of Sydney. He has published poetry in *Landfall*, *Sport*, *Islands*, *Poetry New Zealand* and elsewhere. He has published four volumes of poems, the last being *Bounty* (CUP, 2008). A set of translations into English of selected poems by the Dutch poet Frank Koenegracht with Cold Hub Press will appear in 2014.

Leonard Lambert (1945–) is the author of five collections of verse over as many decades. These include *A Washday Romance* (John McIndoe, 1980), *Park Island* (John McIndoe, 1990), *Natural Anthem* (HeadworX, 2004), *Skywire: Love Poems* (Steele Roberts, 2008), *Remnants* (Steele Roberts, 2013), and a chapbook, *A Morning Walk in the Later Days* (Cold Hub Press, 2010). A talented painter and an accomplished performer of his own work, he lives in Napier with his wife and fellow poet, Jan FitzGerald.

Aleksandra Lane (1977–) is a PhD student at Massey University in Wellington. Her most recent book of poems, *Birds of Clay*, was published by Victoria University Press in 2012, and her work has appeared in various literary magazines, such as *Jacket2*, *Sport*, *Turbine*, *Swamp*, *Snorkel* and *takahē*.

Jessica Le Bas (1954–) won the NZSA Jessie Mackay Award for Best First Book of Poetry in 2008 with her collection *Incognito* (AUP, 2007). Her second collection, *Walking to Africa* (AUP), was released in 2009, and was placed second in the Ashton Wylie Charitable Trust Literature Awards in 2010. She lives in Nelson.

Michele Leggott (1956–) was born in Stratford. She graduated from the University of Canterbury, where she completed a thesis on the poetry of Ian Wedde, and from the University of British Columbia with a PhD on Louis Zukofsky's poetry. She has published seven volumes of poetry. Her first collection, *Like This?* (Caxton, 1988), won the PEN Best First Book of Poetry Award in 1988, and *DIA* (AUP, 1994) won the New Zealand Book Award for Poetry in 1994. Leggott co-founded and edits the New Zealand Electronic Poetry Centre. She has edited and co-edited a number of volumes, including the poems of Robin Hyde — *The Book of Nadath* (AUP, 1999) and *Young Knowledge* (AUP, 2003) — and an anthology of poems from the 1960s and 1970s — *Big Smoke* (AUP, 2000). She was the poetry editor of *Landfall* from 1991 to 1993. Leggott was the New Zealand Poet Laureate from 2008 to 2009 and was made a Member of the New Zealand Order of Merit in 2009. She is currently Professor of English at the University of Auckland.

Graham Lindsay (1952–) was born in Wellington to parents of Scots and English descent. His early influences were a father who read widely, teachers Vaughan Dyer and Miriam Heath, and another who introduced him to the writing of Dylan Thomas. Lindsay has a degree in English and a Diploma of Teaching, and he was the Bethell/Canterbury Writing Fellow in 2004. He was the editor of *Morepork* between 1979 and 1980, and has written six poetry collections, including *The Subject* (AUP, 1994), *Legend of the Cool Secret* (Sudden Valley Press, 1999) and *Lazy Wind Poems* (AUP, 2003). Lindsay lives in England and is working on a novel set in the 1940s.

Anna Livesey (1979–) was born and raised in Wellington and has an MA in Creative Writing from Victoria University. She has won the Macmillan Brown Prize on two occasions and was the Schaeffer Fellow at the Iowa Writers' Workshop in 2003. She has published two collections of poetry, the latest of which is entitled *The Moonmen* (VUP, 2010).

Iain Lonie (1932–1988) was a poet, academic and keen yachtsman, and lectured in classics at the University of Otago. He published six collections of poetry, including the posthumous collection *Winter Walk at Morning* (VUP, 1991).

Rachel McAlpine (1940–) is a poet, novelist and playwright. Her first collection of poetry, *Lament for Ariadne*, was published in 1975 by Caveman Press. She has since published numerous other collections and written several plays and novels. Her non-fiction work includes textbooks on digital communication and books about popular writers.

Robert McLean (1974–) was born in Bethany, Christchurch, and educated at Mairehau High School and at the University of Canterbury. His poetry has appeared in four limited editions: *For the Coalition Dead* (Kilmog Press, 2009), *For Renato Curcio* (Gumtree Press, 2010), *Goat Songs* (Kilmog Press, 2011) and *Graveyard by the Sea* (Cold Hub Press, 2012). In addition to poetry, McLean's essays, journal and periodical articles, reviews and fiction have been widely published. He has lately lived in Lyttelton.

Frankie McMillan (1950–) is a short story writer and poet. Her short story collection *The Bag Lady's Picnic and Other Stories* was published by Shoal Bay Press in 2001. In 2005 she was awarded the Creative New Zealand Todd Bursary. In 2008 and 2009 her work was selected for *Best New Zealand Fiction* anthologies. Many of her stories have also been broadcast on radio. In 2013 she was the winner of the New Zealand Flash Fiction Award. *Dressing for the Cannibals*, a poetry collection, was published in 2009 by Sudden Valley Press, and in that same year she won the New Zealand Poetry Society International Competition. Her recent poetry has appeared in *Turbine*, *JAAM*, *Landfall*, *Trout*, *Snorkel*, *Sport*, *The London Grip*, *Shenandoah* and *Best New Zealand Poems* 2012. In 2014 McMillan is a Bethell writer-in-residence at the University of Canterbury.

CILLA MCQUEEN (1949–) was born in England but has lived in New Zealand since childhood. She now lives in Bluff, Motupohue. McQueen has published 11 collections of poetry, three of which have won New Zealand Book Awards. *A Wind Harp*, her CD of poetry with musical backing that demonstrates her love of performance, was released in 2006. McQueen was the 2009 to 2011 National Library New Zealand Poet Laureate. In 2010 she received the Prime Minister's Award for Literary Achievement in Poetry. Her most recent publication is *Edwin's Egg and other poetic novellas* (OUP, 2014).

MARGARET MAHY (1936–2012) was born in Whakatane. She graduated from the University of Canterbury and from the New Zealand Library School in Wellington. She worked as the children's librarian at Canterbury Public Library before becoming a full-time writer. Mahy published over 120 books in as many as 15 languages. Her numerous awards included the Carnegie Medal and the Hans Christian Andersen Award (both international prizes), the New Zealand Library Association's Esther Glen Medal (six times), the Prime Minister's Award for Literary Achievement in Fiction (2005), an Arts Foundation of New Zealand Icon Award, and several New Zealand Book Awards. In 2009, Tessa Duder edited Mahy's collected poems for children, *The Word Witch* (HarperCollins).

VANA MANASIADIS (1973–) is a Wellington writer of Greek origin whose poetry has appeared in New Zealand literary journals such as *Sport*, *Turbine* and *JAAM*. She grew up in the Wellington suburb of Berhampore, notable at the time for its council flats and colourful locals, and went to school with the grandchildren of Italian fishermen in neighbouring Island Bay. Hector, of 'Hectic Hector', comes from that particular soup of survival and strangeness, and is one of a cast of characters from her collection *Ithaca Island Bay Leaves* (Seraph Press, 2009), which began life as a thesis for a Master of Arts in Creative Writing at Victoria University. In 2012, in Athens, she launched ĒLĒ Press, and she has recently resumed work on a new collection, *The Grief Almanac*.

BILL MANHIRE (1946–) was born in Invercargill and studied at the University of Otago and University College, London. He has published many volumes of poetry and short stories, a collection of essays and interviews (*Doubtful Sounds*, VUP, 1999), and has edited various anthologies, including *121 New Zealand Poems* (Godwit, 2005) and *The*

Wide White Page: Writers Imagine Antarctica (VUP, 2004). He founded the influential Creative Writing Programme at Victoria University. His *Selected Poems* (2012) are published in New Zealand by Victoria University Press and in the UK by Carcanet.

Selina Tusitala Marsh (1971–) is of Samoan, Tuvaluan, English and French descent. She was the first Pacific Islander to graduate with a PhD in English from the University of Auckland and is now a lecturer in the university's English department, specialising in Pasifika literature. She is the co-ordinator of Pasifika Poetry Web, a sister-site of the New Zealand Electronic Poetry Centre. Her first collection, the bestselling *Fast Talking PI* (AUP, 2009), won the NZSA Jessie Mackay Award for Best First Book of Poetry in 2010. Marsh represented Tuvalu at the London Olympics Poetry Parnassus event in 2012, and her work has been translated and has appeared in numerous forms in schools, museums, parks, billboards, print and online literary journals. Her second collection, *Dark Sparring* (2013), is AUP's first enhanced ebook of poetry.

Courtney Sina Meredith (1986–) has a degree in English and Political Studies from the University of Auckland, where she co-edited *Spectrum 5*. Meredith launched her first book of poetry, *Brown Girls in Bright Red Lipstick* (Beatnik, 2012), at the 2012 Frankfurt Book Fair; her play *Rushing Dolls* was published in the same year by Playmarket. Meredith was the Bleibtreu Berlin writer-in-residence in 2011, and she also featured in the International Literature Festival Berlin. Meredith has established a local and international reputation as a performer, poet, musician and playwright. Her work is an on-going discussion of contemporary urban life with an underlying Pacific *politique* and an educated, politically aware, international voice.

Karlo Mila (1974–) was born in Rotorua and is of Tongan, Samoan and Palagi descent. She was educated at Massey University and has published two collections of poetry, the first of which, *Dream Fish Floating* (Huia, 2005), won the NZSA Jessie Mackay Award for Best First Book of Poetry in 2006. She has worked as a teacher and a health research manager. Mila has a PhD in Sociology and is currently a postdoctoral research fellow at the University of Auckland. She lives in Wellington.

David Mitchell (1940–2011) was born in Wellington. His first collection of poems, *Pipe Dreams in Ponsonby*, was published in 1972 by Caveman Press, and although he wrote and performed extensively, his next book, *Steal Away Boy: Selected Poems of David Mitchell* (AUP), did not appear until 2010. Mitchell founded Auckland's Poetry Live! in 1980 and ran it for three years. He completed a BA at Victoria University in 2002.

HARVEY MOLLOY (1961–) is a Wellington poet, editor and teacher who was born in Oldham, England. 'The Battle of San Romano' is from his first book of poems, *Moonshot* (Steele Roberts, 2008). His poetry has appeared in many New Zealand publications, including *Best New Zealand Poems*, *Blackmail Press*, *Brief*, *JAAM*, *Landfall*, *New Zealand Listener*, *Poetry New Zealand*, *Snorkel* and *takahē*. He has recently completed a new book of poems.

ELIZABETH NANNESTAD (1956–) lives in Auckland and has worked as a forensic psychiatrist, then a home-schooling mother. Her latest poetry collection is *Wild Like Me* (VUP, 2013). She is the author of two previous books: *Jump* (AUP, 1986), which was joint winner of the New Zealand Book Award for Poetry, and *If He's a Good Dog He'll Swim* (AUP, 1996).

EMMA NEALE (1969–) was born in Dunedin, graduated BA (First Class Honours) in English from Victoria University, and holds a PhD in English Literature from University College, London. She has published four collections of poetry and five novels and has edited several poetry anthologies, including the parenthood-themed *Swings and Roundabouts* (Godwit, 2008). She edited *Best New Zealand Poems* 2004. Neale won the Todd New Writers' Bursary in 2000 and received the inaugural NZSA Janet Frame Memorial Award for Literature in 2008. Her collection *The Truth Garden* (OUP, 2012) won the Kathleen Grattan Award for Poetry in 2011 and she was the University of Otago Burns Fellow in 2012. Neale works as a freelance writer, editor and creative writing tutor.

JOHN NEWTON (1959–) was born in Blenheim. He grew up on a sheep farm in the Marlborough Sounds, and went to boarding school and university in Christchurch. He has a PhD in English from the University of Melbourne, and has taught at Melbourne and at the University of Canterbury. He is the author of *The Double Rainbow: James K. Baxter, Ngati Hau and the Jerusalem Commune* (VUP, 2009), and three volumes of poetry: *Tales from the Angler's Eldorado* (Untold Books, 1985), *Lives of the Poets* (VUP, 2010) and *Family Songbook* (VUP, 2013). He has also released a CD, *Love Me Tender*, with his country band, The Tenderizers. He now lives on Waiheke Island.

JAMES NORCLIFFE (1946–) has published a collection of short stories, eight collections of poetry — most recently, *Villon in Millerton* (AUP, 2007) and *Shadow Play* (Proverse, 2012) — and several award-winning novels for young people, including *The Loblolly Boy* (Longacre, 2009) and its successor, *The Loblolly Boy and the Sorcerer* (Longacre, 2011). His most recent book for young people is *Felix and the Red Rats* (Longacre, 2012). He had a long-time involvement with *takahē* magazine and has edited anthologies of poetry and writing by young people. He is poetry editor for the Christchurch *Press*. Norcliffe has won a number of awards for both his poetry and his writing for young people. With Bernadette Hall he was presented with a *Press* Literary Liaisons Honour Award in 2003 for lasting contribution to literature in the South Island. He has been awarded writing fellowships both in New Zealand and overseas, including the Burns Fellowship, the IWP/Iowa Residency, and residencies in Hobart, and at Massey University and the University of Otago College of Education. He publishes poetry widely internationally, and regularly reads at festivals and events throughout New Zealand and overseas: most recently the Queensland Poetry Festival in 2008; in Medellin, Colombia, for the International Poetry Festival in 2010; and in 2011 at the Trois-Rivières International Poetry Festival in Quebec.

GREGORY O'BRIEN (1961–) was born in Matamata. He is a painter, poet, essayist, art curator and editor. He has published numerous volumes of poetry, a novel, a novella and many works of non-fiction, including monographs on Ralph Hotere, Euan MacLeod, Pat Hanly and Graham Percy. He is the author of two multi-award-winning art books for children: *Welcome to the South Seas* (AUP, 2004) and *Back and Beyond: New Zealand Painting for the Young and Curious* (AUP, 2008); a book of essays, *After Bathing at Baxter's* (VUP, 2002); and a book about the *School Journal*, *A Nest of Singing Birds* (Learning Media, 2007), which won the reference and anthology category at the 2008 Montana New Zealand Book Awards. He has co-edited a number of books, including the love poetry anthology *My Heart Goes Swimming* (Godwit, 1996), *Big Weather: Poems of Wellington* (Mallinson Rendel, 2009) and *The Oxford Anthology of New Zealand Poetry in English* (1997).

JOHN O'CONNOR (1949–) has specialised in verse satire, haiku and renga (original and in translation), free verse, working-class verse, and the prose poem. His poems have been published widely in New Zealand and overseas. He has published ten books of poems, the most recent being: *Parts of the Moon: Selected Haiku* (Post Pressed, 2007), *Cornelius and*

Co: Collected Working Class Verse (Post Pressed, 2010), *Bright the Harvest Moon* (Poets Group, 2011), and *Aspects of Reality* (HeadworX, 2013). *Whistling in the Dark* will be published by HeadworX in 2014. O'Connor lives in Christchurch with his wife, Sandra.

MARIS O'ROURKE (1940–) has been published in a range of journals in New Zealand and overseas. She has been well placed in competitions including the Caselberg, Robert Burns, Kathleen Grattan Prize, Kevin Ireland and Matariki. O'Rourke has been a guest poet in *Poetry New Zealand* and *a fine line* and her work was included in the play *Aotearoa Found in Translation*. Her first children's book, *Lillibutt's Big Adventure,* was published in 2012 by Duck Creek Press, and her first poetry collection, *Singing With Both Throats,* was published in 2013 by David Ling. Her second children's book will be published in 2014. O'Rourke has performed her work widely, including at the Fringe Festival's 'spit.it.out', the Auckland Writers and Readers Festival, the National Flash Fiction Festival and the Hawke's Bay National Poetry Conference.

PETER OLDS (1944–) was born in Christchurch and lives in Dunedin. He was the University of Otago Burns Fellow in 1978, and received a Janet Frame Literary Trust Award in 2005. His most recent book, *Under the Dundas Street Bridge*, was published by Steele Roberts in 2012. His many books include: *Music Therapy* (Earl of Seacliff, 2001), *Poetry Reading at Kaka Point* (Steele Roberts, 2006) and *Ballad of the Last Cold Pie* (Cold Hub Press, 2010). His poems have appeared in *Big Smoke*, *Landfall* and the *Otago Daily Times*. His *Selected Poems* (with an introduction by Ian Wedde) will be published by Cold Hub Press in 2014.

BOB ORR (1949–) was born in Hamilton and has worked as a boatman. He enrolled briefly at the University of Auckland in 1967 and was a vital part of poetry associated with the university's literary society magazine *Freed* and Arthur Baysting's *Young New Zealand Poets* (Heinemann, 1973). He has published eight volumes of poetry and appeared in various anthologies.

CHRIS ORSMAN (1955–) was born in Lower Hutt. He studied architecture at the University of Auckland and later took Victoria University's Creative Writing Programme. His first collection of poetry, *Ornamental Gorse* (VUP, 1994), won the NZSA Jessie Mackay Award for Best First Book of Poetry in 1995; his second collection, *South* (VUP, 1996), was shortlisted for the Montana New Zealand Book Awards and published in an expanded British edition. *The Lakes of Mars*

(AUP, 2008) was shortlisted for the awards in 2009. In 1988, Orsman established Pemmican Press to publish new voices. He was an Arts Fellow on the Artists to Antarctica Programme in 1997 and Victoria University's writer-in-residence at the International Institute of Modern Letters in 2002. He has published several other volumes of poetry.

VINCENT O'SULLIVAN (1937–) was born in Auckland, and when he retired was teaching at Victoria University. As well as poetry, he has written novels, short stories, plays, biography, libretti and a range of academic publications. His *Requiem for the Fallen*, written with composer Ross Harris, was performed at the 2014 New Zealand Arts Festival by the New Zealand String Quartet and the New Zealand Chamber Choir. A new collection of short stories, *The Families*, and his *Selected Poems* (both VUP) will appear in 2014.

ALISTAIR PATERSON (1929–) was made an Officer of the New Zealand Order of Merit (ONZM) for services to literature in 2006. He edited the literary magazines *Mate* and *Climate* between 1972 and 1982 and *Poetry New Zealand* for 20 years. He has nine books of poetry to his credit, including his fifth long poem, *Africa*, published in 2008 by Puriri Press. A tenth collection is in preparation. His work includes a chapbook on poetic theory, a novel, and two anthologies. He has won the Katherine Mansfield Short Story Award, was co-winner of the University of Auckland's John Cowie Reid Memorial Award for longer poems, and has been a long-time mentor (from 1972) for both tyro and more experienced poets.

KIRI PIAHANA-WONG (1977–) is a New Zealander of Māori (Ngāti Ranginui), Chinese and Pākehā ancestry. She is a poet, editor and publisher. Her first poetry collection, *Night Swimming* (Anahera Press), was published in 2013.

SUGU PILLAY (1946–) was born and raised in Malaysia. Pillay has postgraduate degrees from Victoria University and the University of London. She has taught ESL/ESOL in Malaysia, Singapore, Hong Kong, Melbourne and Christchurch. Awarded a Creative New Zealand grant in 1997, she completed a collection of short fiction, *The Chandrasekhar Limit and other stories*, which was published by the Auckland Writers Group in 2002. In 2009 her play *Serendipity* premiered in Wellington. Her second play, *Salaam Pukekohe*, was co-winner of Playmarket's 2010 Write Out Loud Award. Her collection of poems *Flaubert's Drum* was published in 2012 by Interactive Publications in Australia. Pillay lives in Christchurch.

Mark Pirie (1974–) is a Wellington writer, poetry archivist for PANZA and publisher at HeadworX. He co-founded and edited *JAAM* magazine and currently edits *Broadsheet: New New Zealand Poetry*. His prolific output includes more than 20 volumes of his own poems, and his work has been published in ten countries outside New Zealand. His cricket poetry anthology, *A Tingling Catch* (HeadworX, 2010), received international attention.

Vivienne Plumb (1955–) writes poetry, fiction and drama. She has held the Sargeson Fellowship and a Creative New Zealand/University of Iowa residency, and has been a recipient of the Hubert Church Prose Award for Fiction and the Bruce Mason Playwriting Award. She is a Doctor of Creative Arts (University of Wollongong, Australia), and holds a 2014 Bethell residency at the University of Canterbury. She has published two chapbooks and five collections of poetry.

Lindsay Pope (1949–) was born in Dunedin and currently lives in Nelson. During 2009, as part of his MA thesis at the International Institute of Modern Letters, he wrote a sequence of poems that have their genesis in the human history of the Auckland Islands. 'Outpost' comes from that collection.

Jenny Powell (1960–) is a poet and teacher based in Dunedin. She is a graduate of John Dolan's poetry class at the University of Otago, and has published five poetry collections. These include two collaborative works, *Double Jointed* (Inkweed, 2003) with ten poets, and *Locating the Madonna* (Seraph Press, 2004) with Anna Jackson.

Joanna Preston (1972–) was born in Sydney and grew up in outback New South Wales. She emigrated to Christchurch in 1994. She has an MPhil in Creative Writing from the University of Glamorgan (Wales), and has been widely published in New Zealand and internationally. In 2008 she was the inaugural winner of the Kathleen Grattan Award for Poetry with her debut collection, *The Summer King* (OUP, 2009).

Chris Price (1962–) has an MA in English and German from the University of Auckland, and in Creative Writing from Victoria University. She edited the literary journal *Landfall* from 1993 to 2000, and co-ordinated the New Zealand Post Writers and Readers Week in Wellington from 1992 to 2004. She has published two volumes of poetry, with her first collection, *Husk* (AUP, 2002), winning the NZSA

Jessie Mackay Award for Best First Book of Poetry in 2002. The cross-genre work *Brief Lives* (AUP, 2006) was shortlisted in the biography category of the Montana New Zealand Book Awards in 2007, and she was among the writers and physicists who collaborated on the anthology *Are Angels OK?* (VUP, 2006). Price co-convenes the MA Creative Writing Programme at the International Institute of Modern Letters. In 2011 she was the recipient of the New Zealand Post Mansfield Prize.

John Pule (1962–) is a poet, novelist and artist. He was born in Liku, Niue, and arrived in New Zealand in 1964. He began writing in 1980 after reading the works of New Zealand poets. Pule's novels, poetry and solo exhibitions are in essence narratives of history and place. All are extensions to an on-going project to record his family history into an Aotearoa and Pacific context. He lives in Auckland.

Sarah Quigley (1967–) is an award-winning novelist, critic and columnist. She holds a DPhil in Literature from Oxford University. In 1998 she won the Buddle Findlay Sargeson Fellowship, and in 2000 she was the inaugural winner of the Creative New Zealand Berlin Writers' Residency. She has published four novels, a collection of short fiction, a creative writing manual, and two poetry collections. Her novel *The Conductor* (Vintage, 2011) was the number one bestselling fiction title in New Zealand for 21 weeks. It was longlisted for the International IMPAC Dublin Literary Award and shortlisted for the Prix Femina. Her new collection of fiction, *Tenderness*, will be published by Vintage in 2014. Quigley lives and works in Berlin.

Maggie Rainey-Smith (1950–) grew up in Richmond, Nelson, during a time of apples and orchards rather than wine and vineyards. She is the author of two novels, a published poet and a short story writer, as well as a regular book reviewer on Beattie's Book Blog. Her short stories, essays and poetry have been published in *Landfall*, *Sport*, *takahē*, *New Zealand Listener*, *New Zealand Books*, *4th Floor Journal* and on Radio New Zealand. Her website is maggieraineysmith.com and she blogs at acurioushalfhour.wordpress.com. In 1998 she attended one of the first Victoria University undergraduate poetry workshops led by Gregory O'Brien.

Richard Reeve (1976–) has published four collections of poetry: *Dialectic of Mud* (AUP, 2001), *The Life and the Dark* (AUP, 2004), *In Continents* (AUP, 2008) and the book-length poem *The Among*

(Maungatua Press, 2008). His work has appeared widely in New Zealand and overseas, including the *Best New Zealand Poems* anthologies for 2001, 2004, 2007 and 2008. In 2011, with Mick Abbott, Reeve published *Our Wild Heart: The Possibility of Wilderness in Aotearoa New Zealand* (OUP, 2011). Reeve's fifth collection of poetry, *Generation Kitchen*, will be published by Otago University Press in 2015. He is also working on a long poem, 'Grand Comedy', an excerpt of which was published in *Landfall*. Reeve currently works as a lawyer.

Nicholas Reid (1951–) is an Auckland historian, poet, teacher and critic. He runs the weekly book blog Reid's Reader. Since gaining his doctorate, he has had three biographies and three works of general history published. He dabbled in poetry as an adolescent, but began to write poetry seriously only in early middle-age. His first collection was *The Little Enemy* (Steele Roberts, 2011); his sonnet sequence *Persephone and Dis* appeared in 2013; and he has four times guest-edited *Poetry New Zealand*. He is currently preparing a second collection.

Helen Rickerby (1974–) lives in Wellington. Her third collection, *Cinema* (Mākaro Press, 2014), features poems that take films and film-making as their leaping-off point. She is the co-managing editor of the literary magazine *JAAM*, and runs Seraph Press, a boutique publishing company.

Harry Ricketts (1950–) was born in London, went to Oxford University and before coming to New Zealand in 1981 taught at universities in Hong Kong and the UK. He now teaches English Literature and Creative Non-fiction at Victoria University and co-edits the quarterly review journal *New Zealand Books*. He has written or edited 25 books, including a biography of Kipling, nine collections of poems, extended personal essays and various anthologies. In 2010 he published three books: the anthology *The Awa Book of New Zealand Sports Writing* (Awa Press), *99 Ways into New Zealand Poetry* with Paula Green (Vintage), and a group-biography of a dozen WWI poets, *Strange Meetings: The Poets of the Great War* (Chatto & Windus). His most recent collection of poems, *Just Then*, was published by Victoria University Press in 2012. He was the featured poet in *Poetry New Zealand* 47 and *takahē* 80.

Jack Ross (1962–) grew up in Mairangi Bay, Auckland. He has an MA in English from the University of Auckland and a PhD in Comparative Literature from Edinburgh University. He teaches creative writing at Massey University, Albany. Ross has published numerous collections of poetry and fiction, and edited various magazines and anthologies. He co-edited the *New Zealand Poets in Performance* series with Jan Kemp between 2006 and 2008; he guest-edited *Landfall* 214 in 2007; and he co-edited *Myth of the 21st Century: An Anthology of New Fiction* (Reed) with Tina Shaw in 2006. He is the new managing editor of *Poetry New Zealand*, succeeding Alistair Paterson.

Bill Sewell (1951–2003) was born in Athens, Greece, and spent the first part of his childhood in Southern Europe, the Middle East and England. He completed his education in New Zealand and graduated with a PhD in German from the University of Otago. He taught at Otago before taking law at Victoria University. Sewell was the Burns Fellow at Otago from 1981 to 1982, was president of the New Zealand Poetry Society in the early 1990s and co-edited *New Zealand Books* from 1998 to 2002. He published six volumes of poetry and a guide to the Rimutaka Forest Park, and edited various anthologies, including *Essential New Zealand Poems* with Lauris Edmond (Godwit, 2001). In 2003, Sewell was posthumously awarded the inaugural Lauris Edmond Memorial Award for Poetry.

Iain Sharp (1953–) is a poet, columnist, reviewer and critic. He has published several collections of poetry as well as non-fiction, and is a practised performer of his poetry. His non-fiction titles include a history of the Spirit of Adventure Trust; a book about the treasures in the Auckland City Library collection; and a major biography of Charles Heaphy.

Kerrin P. Sharpe (1953–) is a teacher of creative writing and the inaugural winner of the New Zealand Post Creative Writing Teacher's Award from the International Institute of Modern Letters. Her first collection of poems, *Three Days in a Wishing Well*, was published in 2012 by Victoria University Press. A selection of her poems also appeared in *Oxford Poets 2013: An Anthology*, published by Carcanet. Her second collection of poems, *There's a Medical Name for This*, will be published in 2014 by Victoria University Press. Sharpe is currently working on her third collection with the assistance of a literature grant from Creative New Zealand.

Elizabeth Smither (1941–) was born in New Plymouth, where she worked as a librarian. She has published 17 volumes of poetry, five short story collections and five novels. Her many honours include the New Zealand Book Award for Poetry in 1990, for *A Pattern of Marching* (AUP, 1989), and the Montana New Zealand Book Award for Poetry in 2000, for *The Lark Quartet* (AUP, 1999). She was the Te Mata Estate Poet Laureate between 2001 and 2002, and in 2008 she won the Prime Minister's Award for Literary Achievement in Poetry. She received a University of Auckland Literary Fellowship in 1984 and a Queen Elizabeth II Arts Council Scholarship in Letters in 1987 and 1992. Smither edited *Best New Zealand Poems* 2002. Her work has been widely published in Australia, Canada, Britain and the United States.

C. K. Stead (Christian Karlson) (1932–) was born in Auckland. Within eight years of taking a lectureship position, Stead was Professor of English at the University of Auckland, where he established a creative writing course. He took early retirement to concentrate on writing full-time. His academic writing, poetry and novels have gained him an international reputation, with his non-fiction ranging from his influential *The New Poetic: Yeats to Eliot* (AMS Press, 1964) to critical essays published in *Kin of Place: Essays on 20 New Zealand Writers* (AUP, 2002) and *Book Self* (AUP, 2008). His 16 volumes of poetry include *Collected Poems: 1951–2006* (AUP, 2008), which won the reference and anthology category of the Montana New Zealand Book Awards in 2009. He has written 14 books of fiction, including *Mansfield* (Vintage, 2004), a finalist in the Tasmania Pacific Fiction Prize in 2005, and most recently *Risk* (MacLehose, 2012). Stead was named a CBE in 1985, made a Fellow of the Royal Society of Literature in 1995 and an Honorary Visiting Fellow of St John's College at Oxford in 1997, and was awarded an honorary doctorate by the University of Bristol in 2001. He is a Member of the Order of New Zealand, and he received the Creative New Zealand Michael King Writers' Fellowship in 2005 and the Prime Minister's Award for Literary Achievement in Fiction in 2009.

J. C. Sturm (Jacqueline Cecilia) (1927–2009) was born in Opunake and was of Taranaki Māori descent. One of the first Māori women to gain a degree, she graduated with an MA (First Class Honours) in Philosophy from Victoria University. Initially she wrote short fiction, with work appearing in *Numbers*, *Te Ao Hou* and *New Zealand Short Stories: Second Series* (the first Māori to appear in an anthology). Sturm devoted herself to solo-parenting before collecting work for *The House of the Talking*

Cat (Spiral, 1983), which was shortlisted for the New Zealand Book Awards. She then dedicated herself to poetry and published *Dedications* (Steele Roberts, 1996), which received an Honour Award for Poetry in the Montana New Zealand Book Awards in 1997. She published a further volume of poetry and received an honorary doctorate from Victoria University in 2003. Sturm was married to the poet James K. Baxter.

Robert Sullivan (1967–) was born in Auckland and is of Ngāpuhi and Irish Galway descent. He graduated from the University of Auckland with an MA and worked as Associate Professor of English and director of the Creative Writing Programme at the University of Hawai'i. He has published six volumes of poetry in New Zealand and one in the UK. *Jazz Waiata* (AUP, 1990) won the PEN Best First Book of Poetry Award in 1991, and Sullivan has twice been a finalist in the Montana New Zealand Book Award for Poetry. His book *Weaving Earth and Sky: Myths and Legends of Aotearoa* (Random House, 2002) won the supreme award and the non-fiction category of the New Zealand Post Children's Book Awards in 2003. Sullivan was Literary Fellow at the University of Auckland in 1998 and Distinguished Visiting Writer at the University of Hawai'i in 2001. He has co-edited two anthologies of Polynesian writing, the first of which, *Whetu Moana* (AUP/University of Hawai'i Press, 2003) won the reference and anthology category of the Montana New Zealand Book Awards in 2004. He co-edits *Trout* and he co-edited *Best New Zealand Poems* 2006 with his wife, the poet Anne Kennedy. He is now head of the School of Creative Writing at the Manukau Institute of Technology.

Apirana Taylor (1955–) was born in Wellington and is of Te Whānau ā Apanui, Ngāti Porou, Ngāti Ruanui and Pākehā descent. Taylor has published five volumes of poetry, short stories, a novel, plays and criticism. He was active in the Māori theatre co-operative Te Ohu Whakaari. He was awarded fellowships in writing from Massey University in 1996 and the University of Canterbury in 2002. He has also published sound and video recordings. He has taught creative writing and drama at Whitireia Community Polytechnic.

Charlotte Trevella (1992–) began writing poetry at age seven and had her first poem published in the *New Zealand Listener* when she was ten. Charlotte won the Young Australasian Writers' Award in three consecutive years and the New Zealand Poetry Society under-18 competition in 2007, 2008 and 2009. In 2008 she was selected as one of the top 15 youth poets in the world in the Foyle Young Poet of the Year competition run by the

British Poetry Society. In 2009 she won first prize in the New Zealand Post National Schools Poetry Awards, judged by Jenny Bornholdt.

Chris Tse (1982–) was born and raised in Lower Hutt. He studied film and English literature at Victoria University, where he also completed an MA in Creative Writing. His poetry has appeared in a number of journals and anthologies, and in *AUP New Poets 4*. His first full-length collection is *How to Be Dead in a Year of Snakes* (AUP, 2014).

Brian Turner (1944–) lives in the Ida Valley in Central Otago. He has published an eclectic mix of books, including numerous poetry collections and a memoir. His non-fiction titles reflect his passion for sport and his abiding concern for the environment. Turner was the Burns Fellow at the University of Otago in 1984, the writer-in-residence at the University of Canterbury in 1997, the Te Mata Estate New Zealand Poet Laureate from 2003 to 2005, and he received the Prime Minister's Award for Literary Achievement in Poetry in 2009. He was awarded the Commonwealth Prize for Poetry in 1979 for his first collection, *Ladders of Rain* (John McIndoe, 1978), and the New Zealand Book Award for Poetry for *Beyond* (John McIndoe, 1993) and *Just This* (VUP, 2010).

Hone Tuwhare (1922–2008), of Ngāpuhi descent, was born in Kaikohe and initially worked as a boilermaker. After his bestselling debut in 1964 with *No Ordinary Sun*, Tuwhare published 12 further collections, all well received. He was the University of Otago Burns Fellow twice (1969 and 1974), was awarded honorary doctorates from the universities of Otago and Auckland, was the University of Auckland Literary Fellow in 1991, and the Te Mata Estate Poet Laureate from 1999 to 2000. He received the Prime Minister's Award for Literary Achievement in Poetry in 2003, and was made an Arts Foundation of New Zealand Icon Artist in the same year. Tuwhare won the Montana New Zealand Book Award for Poetry in 1998 and 2002, for *Shape-Shifter* and *Piggy-Back Moon* respectively.

Tim Upperton (1961–) had his first poetry collection, *A House on Fire* (Steele Roberts), published in 2009. He won the Bronwyn Tate Memorial International Poetry Competition in 2011, and the Caselberg Trust International Poetry Competition in 2012 and 2013. His poems have been published widely, including in *Landfall*, *Sport*, *Agni*, *Shenandoah*, *New Zealand Listener* and *North & South*, and anthologies such as *The Best of Best New Zealand Poems* (VUP, 2011), *Villanelles* (Everyman, 2012), and *Sestinas in the Twenty-First Century* (University Press of New England, 2014).

RAE VARCOE (1944–) was brought up in Dunedin and now lives in Nelson. She was formerly an Auckland City Hospital physician and has had a lifelong poetry reading habit. Her poetry writing began in 1997 at the age of 52, when she completed an MA in Creative Writing at Victoria University. *Tributary* was published in 2007 by Victoria University Press, and in 2014 she was shortlisted for the Kathleen Grattan Award.

LOUISE WALLACE (1983–) was born in Gisborne, and has published two collections of poems through Victoria University Press: *Since June* (2009) and *Enough* (2013). Wallace holds an MA in Creative Writing from Victoria University and spent several years teaching creative writing at Massey University, Wellington, and the Nelson Marlborough Institute of Technology. Her poems have appeared in various journals in New Zealand, Australia and Germany, and also featured in the 2011 anthology *The Best of Best New Zealand Poems* (VUP). She lives in Wellington.

IAN WEDDE (1946–) was born in Blenheim and graduated from the University of Auckland with an MA (Honours) in English. Wedde worked as a poetry critic for *London Magazine* and was then awarded the Burns Fellowship at the University of Otago in 1972. His first novel, *Dick Seddon's Great Dive* (R. Dudding, 1976) won the New Zealand Book Award for Fiction in 1977, and a poetry collection, *Spells for Coming Out* (AUP, 1977), was co-winner of the National Book Award for Poetry in 1978. His most recent collection, *The Lifeguard* (AUP, 2013), was a finalist in the 2013 New Zealand Post Book Awards. He spent a number of years as concept leader for art at the Museum of New Zealand Te Papa Tongarewa. A prolific critic, novelist, essayist and poet, Wedde has published six novels and 15 poetry collections, and has co-edited anthologies — including *The Penguin Book of New Zealand Verse* (1985) and *The Penguin Book of Contemporary New Zealand Poetry* (1989). He received the Katherine Mansfield Memorial Fellowship in 2005 and a New Zealand Arts Foundation Laureateship in 2006. He was New Zealand Poet Laureate between 2011 and 2013. In 2013 he was awarded the Creative New Zealand Writers' Residency in Berlin.

MAUALAIVAO ALBERT WENDT (1939–) was born in Samoa and is of the Aiga Sa-Maualaivao, the Aiga Sa-Su'a, and the Aiga Sa-Patu. He is now Emeritus Professor at the University of Auckland, where he was Professor of English from 1988 to 2006. Before that he was principal of Samoa College and Pro-Vice Chancellor of the University of the South Pacific. He has published six collections of poetry, a play, seven novels, and four collections of short stories. He has edited a number of significant anthologies, including the award-winning *Whetu Moana* (AUP/University of Hawai'i Press, 2003) with Reina Whaitiri and Robert Sullivan. He has won many literary prizes, including for his verse novel, *The Adventures of Vela* (Huia, 2009), which won the Commonwealth Writers Prize for the Asia Pacific Region in 2010. Wendt has been awarded numerous honours, including New Zealand's Senior Pacific Islands Artist Award in 2003, Japan's Nikkei Asia Prize for Culture in 2004, the Prime Minister's Award for Literary Achievement in Fiction in 2012, three honorary doctorates, and in 2013, the Order of New Zealand. He lives with his partner, Reina Whaitiri, in Ponsonby, Auckland, and they have ten mokopuna.

Tom Weston (1958–) has published a number of collections through Steele Roberts, with another currently underway. His poems appear regularly in *Sport* and *Landfall*, and have been collected in several anthologies, including the online series *Best New Zealand Poems*.

Pat White (1944–) is author of several volumes of poetry, including *Drought & Other Intimacies* (Steele Roberts, 1999) and *Planting the Olives* (Frontiers Press, 2004), and a collaboration with artist Catherine Day, *Gnossienne* (Wai-te-ata Press, 2012). His prose memoir essays *How the Land Lies* (VUP) was published in 2010. In 2014 *The Quality of Light*, a biography of West Coast poet and novelist Peter Hooper, will be published by Mākaro Press. White has been awarded residencies at Robert Lord Cottage, Randell Cottage, and in 2012 the Seresin/*Landfall* residency. At present he is working on a 'Selected and New' volume of poetry, and further essays.

Alison Wong (1960–) was raised in Napier. She studied mathematics and later creative writing at Victoria University. She spent several years in China in the 1980s and 1990s, and now lives in Geelong, Australia. Her collection *Cup* (Steele Roberts, 2006) was shortlisted for the NZSA Jessie Mackay Award for Best First Book of Poetry in 2007, and her poems were selected for *Best New Zealand Poems* 2006 and 2007. Wong's novel *As the Earth Turns Silver* (Penguin, 2009) won the New Zealand Post Book Award for Fiction in 2010 and was shortlisted for the Australian Prime Minister's Literary Awards that same year.

SUE WOOTTON (1961–) is a Dunedin-based writer whose publications include a short story collection called *The Happiest Music on Earth* (Rosa Mira Books, 2013) and a children's book called *Cloudcatcher* (Steele Roberts, 2010). Her poetry collections are *Hourglass* (2005), *Magnetic South* (2008) and *By Birdlight* (2011), all published by Steele Roberts, and the limited edition letterpress artisan portfolio book *Out of Shape* (Ampersand Duck, 2013). She has received several awards for her work, and has held the Burns Fellowship at the University of Otago. Her website is suewootton.com.

SONJA YELICH (1965–) was born in Auckland and is of Dalmatian descent. She trained as a teacher and studied literature at the University of Auckland. She was first published in the *AUP New Poets* series and her first solo collection, *Clung* (AUP, 2004), won the NZSA Jessie Mackay Award for Best First Book of Poetry in 2005. Her second collection, *Get Some* (AUP, 2008), was a finalist in the Montana New Zealand Book Awards. She was awarded a Buddle Findlay Sargeson Fellowship in 2010.

ASHLEIGH YOUNG (1983–) is a writer and editor currently living in Wellington. Her first book of poems, *Magnificent Moon* (VUP) was published in 2012. Her essays and poems have appeared in *Sport*, *Landfall*, *Turbine*, *Booknotes*, *Hue & Cry*, and *The Griffith Review*. She blogs at eyelashroaming.com.

KAREN ZELAS (1941–) is a Christchurch writer and former psychiatrist. She won the 2013 Playwrights' Association of New Zealand Playwriting Competition. Her poetry and short fiction have been widely published in New Zealand and also in Australia. Her poetry book, *Night's Glass Table* (Interactive Press, 2012) was selected as the 2012 IP Picks Best First Book by Interactive Publications, Brisbane, which also republished her novel *Past Perfect* (2010) as an ebook. Karen edited the anthology *Crest to Crest: Impressions of Canterbury, Prose and Poetry* (Wily Publications, 2009), and is fiction editor of *takahē* literary magazine.

Acknowledgements

Grateful acknowledgement is made to the following poets and copyright holders for permission to reproduce these poems:

Fleur Adcock, 'Having Sex with the Dead', *Glass Wings* (Wellington: VUP, 2013)
Johanna Aitchison, 'Letters from Japanese Kids', *A Long Ago Girl* (Wellington: VUP, 2007)
Raewyn Alexander, 'Old News Curling in the Sun', *AUP New Poets 1* (Auckland: AUP, 1999)
John Allison, 'Near Death Experience', *Both Roads Taken* (Sudden Valley Press, 1997)
Nick Ascroft, 'The Status of the Night', *From the Author of* (Wellington: VUP, 2000)
Tusiata Avia, 'Wild Dogs Under My Skirt', *Wild Dogs Under My Skirt* (Wellington: VUP, 2004)
Stu Bagby, 'First Dance', *As it was in the beginning* (Wellington: Steele Roberts, 2005)
Hinemoana Baker, 'As a Child', *mātuhi | needle* (Wellington: VUP, 2004)
Serie Barford, 'Mongolian Spots', *Tapa Talk* (Wellington: Huia, 2007)
Sarah Jane Barnett, 'When the Sister Walks', *A Man Runs into a Woman* (Wellington: Hue & Cry Press, 2012)
James K. Baxter, 'Ode to Auckland', *Selected Poems of James K. Baxter*, ed. Paul Millar (Auckland: AUP, 2010)
David Beach, 'Abandoned Novel', *Abandoned Novel* (Wellington: VUP, 2006)
Tony Beyer, 'Cut Lilac', *Dancing Bear* (Canberra: Melaleuca Press, 1981)
Peter Bland, 'Sorry, I'm a stranger here myself . . .', *Let's Meet* (Wellington: Steele Roberts, 2003)
Jenny Bornholdt, 'Villanelle', *Summer* (Wellington: VUP, 2003)
Charles Brasch, 'World Without End', *Home Ground* (Christchurch: Caxton, 1974)
Diana Bridge, 'Jars, Bubble Bowls and Bottle Vases', *Aloe and Other Poems* (Auckland: AUP, 2009)
Bub Bridger, 'A Christmas Wish', *Wild Daisies* (Wellington: Mallinson Rendel, 2005)
Sarah Broom, 'defrost the dog', *Gleam* (Auckland: AUP, 2013). Permission courtesy Michael Gleissner

Amy Brown, 'Baba Yaga', *The Propaganda Poster Girl* (Wellington: VUP, 2008)
Diane Brown, 'Follow Me If You Will', *Learning to Lie Together* (Auckland: Godwit, 2004)
James Brown, 'Needs Work', *Warm Auditorium* (Wellington: VUP, 2012)
Owen Bullock, 'abstractions', *Sometimes the Sky Isn't Big Enough* (Wellington: Steele Roberts, 2010)
Rachel Bush, 'She Is Lost', *The Unfortunate Singer* (Wellington: VUP, 2002)
Kate Camp, 'Personal Effects', *Realia* (Wellington: VUP, 2001)
Alistair Te Ariki Campbell, 'Te Rauparaha in Old Age', *Collected Poems* (Christchurch: Hazard Press, 1996)
Meg Campbell, 'My Countrywoman', *The Better Part* (Christchurch: Hazard Press, 2000)
Gordon Challis, 'Poem for Magda', *Building* (Christchurch: Caxton, 1963)
Janet Charman, 'invigilator', *Cold Snack* (Auckland: AUP, 2007)
Geoff Cochrane, 'The Last of Bashō', *The Bengal Engine's Mango After Glow* (Wellington: VUP, 2012)
Glenn Colquhoun, 'To the girl who stood beside me at the checkout counter of Whitcoulls bookstore in Hamilton on Tuesday', previously published in *New Zealand Listener,* 6 July 2002
Kay McKenzie Cooke, 'Feeding the Dogs', *Feeding the Dogs* (Dunedin: OUP, 2003)
Allen Curnow, 'You Will Know When You Get There', *You Will Know When You Get There: Poems 1970–81* (Auckland, Oxford: AUP, Oxford University Press, 1982). Permission courtesy the copyright holder, Tim Curnow, Sydney
Ruth Dallas, 'Photographs of Pioneer Women', *Collected Poems* (Dunedin: OUP, 2000)
Lynn Davidson, 'Cape Gooseberries', *Tender* (Wellington: Steele Roberts, 2006)
Stephanie de Montalk, 'Concrete', *Animals Indoors* (Wellington: VUP, 2000)
John Dickson, 'sleeper', *Sleeper* (Auckland: AUP, 1998)
Emily Dobson, from *A Box of Bees* (Wellington: VUP, 2005)
Lauris Edmond, 'Late Song', *Late Song* (Auckland: AUP, 2000). Permission courtesy the Estate of Lauris Edmond
Murray Edmond, 'The Cold War', *Fool Moon* (Auckland: AUP, 2004)
David Eggleton, 'Titirangi Considered as Wearable Art', *Fast Talker* (Auckland: AUP, 2006)
Riemke Ensing, 'Hokianga Love Song', *Talking Pictures* (Wellington: HeadworX, 2000)

Rangi Faith, 'Advice to a Colonial Artist', *Rivers Without Eels* (Wellington: Huia, 2001)
Fiona Farrell, 'Fairytale', *The Inhabited Initial* (Auckland: AUP, 1999)
Cliff Fell, 'Alive', *The Adulterer's Bible* (Wellington: VUP, 2003)
Jan FitzGerald, 'Cows Crossing', *On a Day Like This* (Wellington: Steele Roberts, 2010)
Joan Fleming, 'Armchair Talking to the Window', *The Same as Yes* (Wellington: VUP, 2011)
Janet Frame, 'The Place', *The Pocket Mirror* (Christchurch: Pegasus Press, 1968)
Janis Freegard, 'Sapphire', *Kingdom Animalia* (Auckland: AUP, 2011)
Anne French, 'The Lady Fishermen', *Cabin Fever* (Auckland: AUP, 1990)
Rhian Gallagher, 'Salt Water Creek', *Salt Water Creek* (London: Enitharmon Press, 2003)
Denis Glover, 'Towards Banks Peninsula', *Enter Without Knocking* (Christchurch: Pegasus Press, 1964)
Paula Green, 'Two Minutes Westward', *Crosswind* (Auckland: AUP, 2004)
David Gregory, 'The Cruise', *Push* (Port Chalmers: Black Doris Press, 2008)
Bernadette Hall, 'The Lay Sister', *Merino Princess* (Wellington: VUP, 2004)
Michael Harlow, 'And, Yes', *Cassandra's Daughter* (Auckland: AUP, 2005)
Siobhan Harvey, 'Tooth', *Lost Relatives* (Wellington: Steele Roberts, 2011)
Dinah Hawken, 'The Tug of War', *Small Stories of Devotion* (Wellington: VUP, 1991)
Helen Heath, 'Ripple', *Graft* (Wellington: VUP, 2012)
Jeffrey Paparoa Holman, from *The Late Great Blackball Bridge Sonnets* (Wellington: Steele Roberts, 2004)
Ingrid Horrocks, 'Light Between Houses', *Mapping the Distance* (Wellington: VUP, 2010)
John Horrocks, 'Weather Report — Fine', *Raw Places* (Wellington: Steele Roberts, 2005)
David Howard, 'A Simple Chronology', *The In-complete Poems* (Lyttelton: Cold Hub Press, 2011)
Keri Hulme, 'Waiting on the Laughing Owl', *Strands* (Auckland: AUP, 1992)
Sam Hunt, 'My father today', *Knucklebones: Poems 1962–2012* (Nelson: Craig Potton, 2012)
Jan Hutchison, 'Unwinding Matariki's Hair', *The Happiness of Rain* (Wellington: Steele Roberts, 2012)
Kevin Ireland, 'Painting in the Maniototo', *Selected Poems 1963–2013* (Wellington: Steele Roberts, 2013)
Rob Jackaman, 'Lemons (Off Season)', *Buried Ships* (Christchurch: Hazard Press, 1996)

Anna Jackson, 'Badminton', *Thicket* (Auckland: AUP, 2011)
Michael Jackson, 'The Moths', *Penguin Contemporary New Zealand Poetry* (Auckland: Penguin, 1989)
Helen Jacobs, 'Vessel containing', *Lyric Road* (Wellington: Steele Roberts, 2006)
Adrienne Jansen, 'Dunedin: Playing Scrabble with my aunt', *A Stone Seat and a Shadow Tree* (Titahi Bay: Inkweed, 2001)
Louis Johnson, 'The Last Cannibal', *Louis Johnson: Selected Poems* (Wellington: VUP, 2000)
Mike Johnson, 'Up On High', *The Vertical Harp* (Auckland: Titus Books, 2006)
Andrew Johnston, 'The Sunflower', *Sol* (Wellington: VUP, 2007)
Jan Kemp, 'Swimming', *Dante's Heaven* (Auckland: Puriri Press, 2006)
Anne Kennedy, 'I was a feminist in the eighties', *Sing-song* (Auckland: AUP, 2003)
Fiona Kidman, 'Makara Beach, Spring', *Going to the Chathams: Poems, 1977–1984* (Auckland: Heinemann, 1985)
Koenraad Kuiper, from 'Tales', *Timepieces* (Christchurch: Hazard Press, 1999)
Leonard Lambert, 'A Morning Walk in the Later Days', *A Morning Walk in the Later Days* (Lyttelton: Cold Hub Press, 2010)
Aleksandra Lane, 'Sold Out', *Birds of Clay* (Wellington: VUP, 2012)
Jessica Le Bas, 'Two Angels', *Incognito* (Auckland: AUP, 2007)
Michele Leggott, 'Slow Reader', *Mirabile Dictu* (Auckland: AUP, 2009)
Graham Lindsay, 'River of Love', *Lazy Wind Poems* (Auckland: AUP, 2003)
Anna Livesey, 'Autumn Day', *The Moonmen* (Wellington: VUP 2010)
Iain Lonie, 'Proposal at Allans Beach', *Winter Walk at Morning* (Wellington: VUP, 1991)
Rachel McAlpine, 'Before the Fall', *Recording Angel* (Wellington: Mallinson Rendel, 1983)
Robert McLean, 'Springtime in America', previously published in *Poetry New Zealand* 40 (2010)
Frankie McMillan, 'Developing My Father', *Dressing for the Cannibals* (Christchurch: Sudden Valley Press, 2009)
Cilla McQueen, 'Living Here', *Axis* (Dunedin: OUP, 2001)
Margaret Mahy, 'Bubble Trouble', *Bubble Trouble* (London: Frances Lincoln, 2008)
Vana Manasiadis, 'Hectic Hector', *Ithaca Island Bay Leaves* (Wellington: Seraph Press, 2009)
Bill Manhire, 'Kevin', *Lifted* (Wellington: VUP, 2005)

Selina Tusitala Marsh, 'Two Nudes on a Tahitian Beach, *1894*', *Fast Talking PI* (Auckland: AUP, 2009)
Courtney Sina Meredith, 'Homeland', previously published in *Poetry New Zealand* 46 (2013)
Karlo Mila, 'Eating Dark Chocolate and Watching Paul Holmes' Apology', *Dream Fish Floating* (Wellington: Huia, 2005)
David Mitchell, 'A Letter', *Steal Away Boy* (Auckland: AUP, 2010)
Harvey Molloy, 'Battle of San Romano', *Moonshot* (Wellington: Steele Roberts, 2008)
Elizabeth Nannestad, 'Facing the Empty Page', *If He's a Good Dog He'll Swim* (Auckland: AUP, 1996)
Emma Neale, 'Well', *The Truth Garden* (Dunedin: OUP, 2012)
John Newton, 'Opening the book', *Lives of the Poets* (Wellington: VUP, 2010)
James Norcliffe, 'The Gentle Art of Manipulation', *Villon in Millerton* (Auckland: AUP, 2007)
Gregory O'Brien, 'House and Children', *Winter I Was* (Wellington: VUP, 1999)
John O'Connor, 'A Left Hook', *A Particular Context* (Christchurch: Sudden Valley Press, 1999)
Maris O'Rourke, 'On Being Told I'm To Be a Grandmother: a Villanelle', *Singing with Both Throats* (Auckland: David Ling, 2013)
Peter Olds, 'Under the Dundas Street Bridge', *Under the Dundas Street Bridge* (Wellington: Steele Roberts, 2012)
Bob Orr, 'Calypso', *Calypso* (Auckland: AUP, 2008)
Chris Orsman, 'A Colonial Farewell', *South* (Wellington: VUP, 1996)
Vincent O'Sullivan, 'Seeing You Asked', *Seeing You Asked* (Wellington: VUP, 1998)
Alistair Paterson, 'Laying Your Ghost', *Cities and Strangers* (Dunedin: Caveman Press, 1975)
Kiri Piahana-Wong, 'This is it', *Night Swimming* (Auckland: Anahera Press, 2013)
Sugu Pillay, 'St Heliers', *Flaubert's Drum* (Brisbane: Interactive Press, 2012)
Mark Pirie, 'Three Short Films (with "*Landscape*" included)', *Gallery — A Selection* (Cambridge: Salt Publishing, 2003)
Vivienne Plumb, 'Vic's Dick', *Salamanca* (Wellington: HeadworX, 1998)
Lindsay Pope, 'Outpost', previously published in *Swamp*, issue 4
Jenny Powell, 'Love in the Early Winter', *Hats* (Wellington: HeadworX, 2000)
Joanna Preston, 'Parable of the Drought', *The Summer King* (Dunedin: OUP, 2008)

Chris Price, 'Keeping Ravens', *Husk* (Auckland: AUP, 2002)
John Pule, from 'The Hurricane Love Songs', *Burn My Head in Heaven* (Auckland: Penguin, 1998)
Sarah Quigley, 'To Waitemata Harbour', *AUP New Poets 1* (Auckland: AUP, 1999)
Maggie Rainey-Smith, 'At Katherine's Bay', *Eastbourne: An Anthology*, (Wellington: Mākaro Press, 2013)
Richard Reeve, 'Summer Wedding', *In Continents* (Auckland: AUP, 2008)
Nicholas Reid, 'Bluff Seas', *The Little Enemy* (Wellington: Steele Roberts, 2011)
Helen Rickerby, from *Abstract Internal Furniture* (Wellington: HeadworX, 2001)
Harry Ricketts, 'The Necessity of Failure', *Your Secret Life* (Wellington: HeadworX, 2005)
Jack Ross, 'Trying to Write', *To Terezin* (Auckland: Massey University, 2007)
Bill Sewell, 'By Ships We Live', *The Ballad of 51* (Wellington: HeadworX, 2003)
Iain Sharp, 'The Ponsonby Strut', *The Singing Harp* (Paekakariki: Earl of Seacliff Art Workshop, 2004)
Kerrin P. Sharpe, 'Mining the Heart', *Three Days in a Wishing Well* (Wellington: VUP, 2012)
Elizabeth Smither, 'Leaf Flurry Tram', *The Blue Coat* (Auckland: AUP, 2013)
C. K. Stead, 'Deconstructing the Rainbow Warrior', *Collected Poems 1951–2006* (Auckland: AUP, 2008)
J. C. Sturm, 'Honestly', *Dedications* (Wellington: Steele Roberts, 1996)
Robert Sullivan, 'Listen to the Rhythm of the Falling Rain', *Pike Ake!* (Auckland: AUP, 1993)
Apirana Taylor, 'Sad Joke on a Marae', *A Canoe in Midstream* (Christchurch: CUP, 2009)
Charlotte Trevella, 'The Red Dress', *Because Paradise* (Wellington: Steele Roberts, 2009)
Chris Tse, 'In Which the Author Interviews a Dead Man', *How to Be Dead in the Year of Snakes* (Auckland: AUP, 2014)
Brian Turner, 'Just This', *Just This* (Wellington: VUP, 2009)
Hone Tuwhare, 'Deep River Talk', *Deep River Talk: Collected Poems* (Auckland: Godwit, 1993)
Tim Upperton, 'Kindness', *A House on Fire* (Wellington: Steele Roberts, 2009)
Rae Varcoe, 'My Hairdresser', previously published in *Sport* 38, winter 2010

Louise Wallace, 'I feel like I am having the world's heaviest baby', *Enough* (Wellington: VUP, 2013)
Ian Wedde, 'To Art and Praxis', *The Commonplace Odes* (Auckland: AUP, 2001)
Albert Wendt, 'Last Night', *From Mānoa to a Ponsonby Garden* (Auckland: AUP, 2012)
Tom Weston, 'The Sadness of Gifts', *Small Humours of Daylight* (Wellington: Steele Roberts, 2008)
Pat White, 'Learning to Live Outdoors', *Planting the Olives* (Masterton: Frontiers Press, 2004)
Alison Wong, 'there's always things to come back to the kitchen for', *Cup* (Wellington: Steele Roberts, 2006)
Sue Wootton, 'Alpine', *By Birdlight* (Wellington: Steele Roberts, 2011)
Sonja Yelich, 'wires', *Clung* (Auckland: AUP, 2004)
Ashleigh Young, 'Doors', *Magnificent Moon* (Wellington: VUP, 2012)
Karen Zelas, 'Small Islands of Difference', *Night's Glass Table* (Brisbane: Interactive Press, 2012)

About the Editors

Siobhan Harvey is a poet and non-fiction author who has published five books. She has worked as poetry editor of *takahē* magazine and editor of the Poetry Archive (UK), where she worked as assistant director on the 25 New Zealand Poets on the Poetry Archive UK project, which was launched in 2012. She has also been a consulting editor of *International Literary Quarterly* and guest editor of *Poetry New Zealand* and *JAAM*. Graham Beattie once described her as a 'literary activist', a term she actively embraces, especially in her literary organisational work, which has included organising an annual writers' festival series at the Auckland Art Gallery, mentoring six writers into publication through the New Zealand Society of Authors mentorship scheme and, between 2006 and 2013, acting as New Zealand's National Poetry Coordinator. She has written book reviews and literary articles for numerous New Zealand newspapers and journals, including *Landfall*, *New Zealand Listener*, *New Zealand Herald*, *The Press* and Beattie's Book Blog. Harvey is a lecturer and tutor at the Centre of Creative Writing at the Auckland University of Technology AUT.

James Norcliffe is a poet, writer and editor who has published a collection of short stories, eight collections of poetry and several award-winning novels for young people, most recently *Felix and the Red Rats* (Longacre, 2012), which has been shortlisted for the 2014 New Zealand Post Children's Book Awards. He has had a long-time involvement with *takahē* and has edited anthologies of poetry and writing by young people. He is poetry editor for the Christchurch *Press*. Norcliffe has been awarded writing fellowships both in New Zealand and overseas, including the Burns Fellowship, the IWP/Iowa Residency, and residencies in Hobart, at Massey University and at the University of Otago College of Education. He publishes poetry widely internationally, and regularly reads at festivals and occasions throughout New Zealand and overseas.

HARRY RICKETTS teaches English Literature and Creative Non-fiction at Victoria University, and co-edits the quarterly review journal *New Zealand Books*. He has written or edited 25 books, including a biography of Kipling, nine collections of poems, extended personal essays and various anthologies. His most recent collection of poems, *Just Then*, was published by Victoria University Press in 2012, and his essay 'On Masks and Migration: Learning to Stand Upright' appeared in the Griffith Review 43, *Pacific Highways*. He is working on an anthology of New Zealand war writing and writing about friendship.

Index of Titles

A

from 'A Box of Bees' 80
'A Christmas Wish' 46
'A Colonial Farewell' 196
'A Left Hook' 190
'A Letter' 178
'A Morning Walk in the Later Days' 146
'A Simple Chronology' 114
'Abandoned Novel' 37
from 'Abstract Internal Furniture' 229
'abstractions' 54
'Advice to a Colonial Artist' 88
'Alive' 90
'Alpine' 262
'And, Yes' 104
'Armchair Talking to the Window' 92
'As a Child' 30
'At Katherine's Bay' 224
'Autumn Day' 153

B

'Baba Yaga' 30
'Badminton' 125
'Battle of San Romano' 179
'Before the Fall' 158
'Bluff Seas' 228
'Bubble Trouble' 163
'By Ships We Live' 233

C

'Calypso' 195
'Cape Gooseberries' 71
'Concrete' 72
'Cows Crossing' 91
'Cut Lilac' 38

D

'Deconstructing the Rainbow Warrior' 239
'Deep River Talk' 252
'defrost the dog' 48
'Developing My Father' 160
'Doors' 264
'Dunedin: Playing Scrabble with my aunt' 129

E

'Eating Dark Chocolate and Watching Paul Holmes' Apology' 173

F

'Facing the Empty Page' 181
'Fairytale' 89
'Feeding the Dogs' 67
'First Dance' 28
'Follow Me If You Will' 50

H

'Having Sex with the Dead' 21
'Hectic Hector' 166
'Hokianga Love Song' 85
'Homeland' 172
'Honestly' 241
'House and Children' 188

I

'I feel like I am having the world's heaviest baby' 256
'I was a feminist in the eighties' 141
'In Which the Author Interviews a Dead Man' 249
'invigilator' 61

J

'Jars, Bubble Bowls and Bottle Vases' 43
'Just This' 251

K

'Keeping Ravens' 218
'Kevin' 169
'Kindness' 254

L

'Last Night' 258
'Late Song' 81
'Laying Your Ghost' 202
'Leaf Flurry Tram' 238
'Learning to Live Outdoors' 260
'Lemons (Off Season)' 123
'Letters from Japanese Kids' 22
'Light Between Houses' 112
'Listen to the Rhythm of the Falling Rain' 243
'Living Here' 161
'Love in the Early Winter' 215

M

'Makara Beach, Spring' 143
'Mining the Heart' 237
'Mongolian Spots' 31
'My Countrywoman' 59
'My father today' 118
'My Hairdresser' 255

N

'Near Death Experience' 24
'Needs Work' 51

O

'Ode to Auckland' 33
'Old News Curling in the Sun' 23
'On Being Told I'm To Be a Grandmother: a Villanelle' 192
'Opening the book' 185
'Outpost' 213

P

'Painting in the Maniototo' 122
'Parable of the Drought' 216
'Personal Effects' 56
'Photographs of Pioneer Women' 70
'Poem for Magda' 60
'Proposal at Allans Beach' 156

R

'Ripple' 110
'River of Love' 151

S

'Sad Joke on a Marae' 246
'Salt Water Creek' 96
'Sapphire' 94
'Seeing You Asked' 200
'She Is Lost' 55
'sleeper' 78
'Slow Reader' 149
'Small Islands of Difference' 266
'Sold Out' 147
'Sorry, I'm a stranger here myself . . .' 39
'Springtime in America' 159
'St Heliers' 206

'Summer Wedding' 226
'Swimming' 140

T
from 'Tales' 144
'Te Rauparaha in Old Age' 57
'The Cold War' 82
'The Cruise' 101
'The Gentle Art of Manipulation' 187
from 'The Hurricane Love Songs' 222
'The Lady Fishermen' 95
'The Last Cannibal' 134
'The Last of Bashō' 64
from 'The Late Great Blackball Bridge Sonnets' 111
'The Lay Sister' 102
'The Moths' 127
'The Necessity of Failure' 230
'The Place' 93
'The Ponsonby Strut' 235
'The Red Dress' 247
'The Sadness of Gifts' 259
'The Status of the Night' 25
'The Sunflower' 135
'The Tug of War' 107
'there's always things to come back to the kitchen for' 261
'This is it' 204
'Three Short Films (with "*Landscape*" included)' 208
'Titirangi Considered as Wearable Art' 83
'To Art and Praxis' 257
'To the girl who stood beside me at the checkout counter of Whitcoulls bookstore in Hamilton on Tuesday' 65
'To Waitemata Harbour' 223
'Tooth' 105
'Towards Banks Peninsula' 98
'Trying to Write' 232
'Two Angels' 148
'Two Minutes Westward' 99
'Two Nudes on a Tahitian Beach, *1894*' 170

U
'Under the Dundas Street Bridge' 193
'Unwinding Matariki's Hair' 120
'Up On High' 131

V
'Vessel containing' 128
'Vic's Dick' 211
'Villanelle' 42

W
'Waiting on the Laughing Owl' 117
'Weather Report — Fine' 113
'Well' 184
'When the Sister Walks' 32
'Wild Dogs Under My Skirt' 26
'wires' 263
'World Without End' 45

Y
'You Will Know When You Get There' 68

Thanks

The editors wish to acknowledge Lauris Edmond and Bill Sewell. We also wish to acknowledge with gratitude the hard work and support of the team at Random House New Zealand, particularly Nicola Legat and Anna Bowbyes, in helping to bring this book together.

The assistance of Creative New Zealand is gratefully acknowledged by the publisher.

A GODWIT BOOK published by Random House New Zealand, 18 Poland Road, Glenfield, Auckland, New Zealand

For more information about our titles go to www.randomhouse.co.nz

A catalogue record for this book is available from the National Library of New Zealand

Random House New Zealand is part of the Random House Group

New York London Sydney Auckland Delhi Johannesburg

First published 2014

ISBN 978 1 77553 459 4

Cover design: www.areadesign.co.nz
Internal design and photography: Megan van Staden

Printed in China by Everbest Printing Co Ltd